Empowered

cx

Finding Direction for
Genuine Spiritual Leadership

Chris Olson

Dedication

To my wonderful wife, Amy with whom I am blessed to serve in the ministry. You are the epitome of a Proverbs 31 woman and a very powerful voice in church leadership. There are no words to express what you mean to me, and your love and care for me truly exemplify how the bride should love and care for the bridegroom. I love you dearly!

Table of Contents

Acknowledgements

First and Foremost to our one true living God, Jesus — The very reason we exist. Thank you for everything — salvation, love, and the opportunity to worship you. May our lives bring You glory and honor!

To those great apostolic leaders that have paved the way before us leaving a foundation and legacy for our future generations. And, specifically those that have provided me a true example of godly leadership. Whether intentionally through mentorship or unintentionally through your normal leadership practice, you have inspired me greatly with your lives. In particular, those that have had the greatest impact:

- My Bishop, G.A. Mangun (1919-2010) and Vesta Mangun
- Pastor Anthony Mangun and Mickey Mangun
- Pastor David Akers and Rhonda Akers
- Reverend Dennis Durand and Mary Durand

Also, to all those that helped make this book possible including:

- Gentry Needham, cover design
- Geoffrey Stone, editing
- Michael Grossman, interior design and overall formatting

Introduction

"The task of the leader is to get his people from where they are to where they have not been."
— HENRY KISSENGER

L eadership is certainly a hot topic these days. Many in the church view and define leadership as a function of how fast you can grow your church numerically. Furthermore, many conferences bearing the name "Leadership" and all its various forms are generally, and more accurately, church growth conferences aiming to give you the latest techniques in "winning your city." Certainly this has some merit. We should absolutely seek to advance the kingdom of God at all costs. However, I am afraid that this paradigm of leadership gives birth to a false premise on what leadership truly is.

Leadership is much more than growing numbers. Now, don't stone me just yet, but leadership is more than *just* seeing people get baptized and filled with the Holy Ghost. In fact, in many areas leadership in the church has more to do with what you do with people *after* they are saved than it does getting them saved. It is from this premise that I write *Empowered: Finding Direction for Genuine Spiritual Leadership.*

∽

Empowered

As spiritual leaders, we are all empowered by God to bring people out of bondage and darkness and into His marvelous light. We would think that this statement applies only to getting people saved, but there is more to the story. Over the course of a lifetime, a person may experience different forms of bondage and darkness even after they have been serving God for years. It is our job to use the power that God has given us to reel them back in and help them refocus.

Notice the word *empower*. It generally means that someone has given power to another. As leaders, we have been empowered and commissioned by God. But how we use that power can make or break us in the quest toward genuine spiritual leadership. There are proper ways to exercise the power that God has given you. This book looks at the definition of power as it appears in the practice of traditional leadership. We will explore the five forms of leadership power: expert, coercive, reward, referent, and legitimate.

ഊ

Direction

Leadership involves direction. Specifically, leaders must hone in on, through much prayer and fasting, the direction in which the congregation should go, get there themselves, and then call the others to where they are before moving on again. This is a wash, rinse, and repeat cycle that keeps everyone moving in the same direction. This is key since our ultimate destination is heaven. It is a strait gate and a narrow way (see Matthew 7:14).

The path to heaven doesn't move. It is found in the Bible, our road map. Through the lens of the

Word of God, the leader discerns the direction for the people and begins the journey, never wavering to the right hand or the left. Sure, there will be obstacles, but leaders must successfully navigate these and stay the course.

∽

Disclaimer

Before we go any further, let me stress that the principles and teachings in this book have been part of a very successful and fully vetted research study on how leadership is manifested across many different cultures of the world. (For more on this study, please see the books in the References and Further Study section at the end of the book.)

It is not my intention to demean or stereotype any race or culture. Our different races, ethnicities, and cultures are some of the most wonderful things about God's great creation. And, we know also that when the Holy Ghost comes into a person's heart, they are transformed into a new creature and are no longer boxed-in to past traditional and cultural norms. They become free to use whatever cultural artifacts they inherently possess for the glory of God.

However, we would also be naive to think that culture does not play a major part in shaping one's thinking. For instance, the Hebrew word for God is *El*. However, in the Spanish language, *el* is only an article. This does not make God any bigger or smaller respectively, nor does it suggest blasphemy of any kind. Obviously, such things as these are culturally driven. So, it is important to note that when I make a cultural reference, it is only for the purpose of finding a correlation between it and traditional leadership style and then to cross that correlation with what the Bible teaches using types and symbols.

All of this is to say, I hope you will keep everything in perspective and take it with a gracious spirit. I hope you enjoy reading this book, and my heart-felt prayer is that it blesses you in some way. I humbly believe that it contains timeless principles that will foster genuine and powerful spiritual leadership. The undeniable side effect of this kind of leadership is church growth, not just in numbers alone but also in spirit, love, and dedication, which cannot be valued.

Chapter One

Leadership: Misconceptions and Its True Identity

"If your actions inspire others to dream more, learn more, do more and become more, you are a leader"
— JOHN QUINCY ADAMS

O ver the course of the last century, the subject of leadership has intrigued scholars and intellectuals alike, provoking research in a quest to define its very essence. However, its conception is as old as time, if you view the creation story as an act of leadership. Certainly, the quality and characteristic of innovation comes to mind when discussing the subject. And so, it is fitting to describe God as the ultimate Leader when recounting how He flung the stars into existence and created everything from nothing.

You see, that's what leaders *do*. They create; they innovate. And in so doing, they inspire others to accomplish similar acts that the ordinary dare not attempt. Moreover, the most exceptional spiritual leaders understand that since we are created in God's image, then at least some of His creative power has been imparted to us.

Spiritual leaders are those innovators that let the Holy Ghost lead through them. True leadership can manifest itself in many ways and several different levels. For example, the pastor of a church fulfills the office of leader as he pours wisdom into his lay ministers. Likewise, the Sunday school teacher, who is barely recognized for her powerful contribution to the kingdom, fulfills the office of leader every time she ministers and serves her students. On an even deeper level, you can be a leader "from the pew" in soul winning or worship in the congregation of your church.

Wherever you find yourself leading or aspiring to lead, it is absolutely paramount and essential that you depend on God for wisdom, guidance, and favor. Leaders focused on the growth and development of people for the propagation of the gospel must depend on Him or risk eventually falling away. Anything short of this will not suffice in the spiritual realm. Leadership in secular organizations can get away with selfish and self-serving motives because sadly the whole system, in many ways, is built to allow it!

However, the kingdom of God operates on a completely different level than the world. Isaiah states, "For my thoughts are not your thoughts, neither are your ways my ways, saith the LORD. For as the heavens are higher than the earth, so are my ways higher than your ways, and my thoughts than your thoughts" (Isaiah 55:8-9). God told Isaiah that His thoughts and intentions are on a completely different level. Human beings cannot even conceive them! Therefore, it is imperative that spiritual leaders commit fully to being *led* by the Holy Ghost before they attempt to *lead* anyone else. Furthermore, that commitment must be renewed daily to maximize success.Sadly, many spiritual leaders fail because they failed to learn this lesson first. It is my sincere prayer that all leaders, aspiring and otherwise, who read this book would learn to commit fully to being led by the Holy Ghost now before it is too late. Now, let's address two common misconceptions that influence spiritual leadership. This will help to cultivate the main message of the forthcoming chapters.

ဏာ

Leadership is Position
Unfortunately, some people have a distorted view of leadership, one that is more authoritarian than servant-like. Those people esteem the position as the pinnacle of life and have no intention or ability to develop others and lead them to greatness in God.

However, real leaders seek a much deeper, more powerful telos and look beyond status. True leaders are more concerned about developing others and leading *them* to the pinnacle of success and have little time for the shallow pursuit of personal gain and mere titles. There is something to be said of the pursuit of a title. The Italian Renaissance philosopher Niccolò Machiavelli declared that "titles do not honor men, men honor titles."

Machiavelli is not what we would describe as a "role model" for spiritual leadership. In fact, history records him as being a very wicked man that pursued absolute power. However, why is it that such a wicked man could grasp one of the most powerful truths of leadership while Spirit-filled individuals still struggle with it?

It is sad, and quite frankly disgraceful, for Holy Ghost–filled children of God to get so bent out of shape about a position or title. I have heard people in the church make statements like "if pastor would only give me a position" or "why do I even bother when I don't get any recognition". I've got news for you, sir and ma'am alike: True leadership, especially spiritual leadership, has never been nor will it ever be defined by the overrated and extremely shallow nouns and adjectives used to describe one's office! True and powerful leadership is defined by your actions and whether or not those actions edify the body of Christ and bring God glory. Respect is not deserved — it's earned.

Yes, according to the Word of God, we must respect the authority, both spiritual and secular, that God has placed in our lives. Yet, respect for the person that holds the authority works differently. That respect, the kind that will rally others to your side when times get rough, is earned and not automatic. We are mandated by God to respect you because of the office you hold, but not the way that you hold the office! This principle makes all the difference in the world when it comes to spiritual leadership. Instead of focusing on titles and positions that cause men and women to drown in shallow waters, we must focus on the purpose behind those positions: adding value to people's lives and leading them closer to God in the process. The ironic part about leading like this is that type of action does not require a formal office at all.

If you feel called to lead, then it is simple, lead. Quit waiting for a position or title to do so. Proverbs 18:16 states, "A man's gift maketh room for him, and bringeth him before great men." If it is God's plan and will for you to be a leader, then you will excel if you take the initiative and not wait to be appointed to some office. You can lead in the context of where you are physically right now! Of course, I recommend that you discuss your feelings with your pastor. I am sure he will pray with you for direction and help you to get more involved in your church. However, please do not make the mistake of equating leadership with some kind of position because this attitude is the beginning of sorrows and frustration for aspiring leaders.

Leaders in the kingdom of God are stewards of the lives that God has entrusted in their care. The word *steward*, and its derivatives, is found many times in the Word of God, and every time it is mentioned it describes a person who has been entrusted with the care of something that was not originally theirs. Leaders in the kingdom of God are servants that have been assigned the task of taking care of and developing their followers for the Lord. Consider the parable of the talents that Jesus so eloquently delivered to his followers:

> For the kingdom of heaven is as a man travelling into a far country, who called his own servants, and delivered unto them his goods. And unto one he gave five talents, to another two, and to another one; to every man according to his several ability; and straightway took his journey. (Matthew 25:14-15)

Most of us know the rest of the story. The first *steward* was given five talents and invested them in some venture, essentially doubling that which he was originally given. Likewise, the next *steward* was given two talents and doubled his lot as well. However, the last *steward* selfishly and without faith buried his one and only talent in the ground. He sat on it! He misused what the master had entrusted to him. The interesting thing is that the master originally chose this man because he saw something in him. The Bible says that the master gave to every one of them according to their own ability. He knew that if the man would apply himself correctly and responsibly, then he would be successful. However, he failed. He failed most likely because he looked at how much the master gave the other two stewards. He took his eyes off of the task and set them on position and prestige. If you only get one piece of information out of this book, then please let it be this: "YOU DON'T NEED A POSITION TO BE A LEADER."

If you are in a leadership position right now, are you working to develop the people that God has entrusted in your care? Are you investing in them? Are you pouring into them? If you are not, then you may end up like that wicked servant that selfishly sat on the talent that was given him. The master cast him into outer darkness and gave his talent (or *people* for the purpose of this exercise) to another, more capable *steward* (or leader). Also, let this be a warning to all those who desire a position. Leadership is not a game. You are dealing with and entrusted with the souls of God's elect! James 3:1 declares, "My brethren, be not many masters, knowing that we shall receive the greater condemnation." We will be judged for the way that we lead others.

If you desire a position only, then you do not have the heart for leadership. Please, for your own sake and for the sake of those you would be steward of, do not seek leadership. Seek the will of God and a heart for the development of people, and God will place you exactly where He wants you to be when He wants you to be there.

This is fundamental to leadership. If you can't grasp this, then you need not go any further in your pursuit of a spiritual office because you will find yourself to be continually frustrated at your lack of progress. Jesus made it clear that those desiring only a position will be abased, which means to be lowered (see Matthew 23:12)! True leadership comes from God's anointing, but He can't fill someone that is already full of themselves!

സ

Leaders Are Born Not Made

Another common misconception about leadership is that leaders are born with all of the inherent traits to be successful. Although many great leaders have been blessed by being born with charisma, communication skills, and other popular leadership traits, it is more common that leaders have to learn how to be effective and successful.

Originally, the popular line or mode of thinking was that leaders are born with inherent traits. Some have it and some don't. As depressing as this idea may be, it is only partially right. Yes, some people just seem to be born to lead, as they inherently possess many of the traits and characteristics necessary for successful leadership. However, that does not mean that leadership has to be isolated to only a few. You can, with dedicated prayer, fasting, study, and a genuine call from God, be a successful leader in His kingdom.

Although somewhat outside of the scope of this work, I feel it necessary to delve into at least some of the history of popular leadership thought and scholarship in order to construct a framework on which to build the remaining subject matter.

The Trait Approach

Leadership traits captured the attention of scholars in the early twentieth century. The theories developed from the trait approach were dubbed the *great man theories* because researchers identified inherent characteristics that made great leaders. In terms of spiritual leadership, there has only ever been one "great man" to have existed since the inception of the universe, namely Jesus Christ. However, I do understand and appreciate the work of these researchers and agree that it is necessary to understand how good leadership manifests itself. Over the course of the whole twentieth century, five key common leadership characteristics were derived from the collective research—all of which are absolutely applicable to spiritual leadership.

Intelligence

The trait of intelligence was found to be positively correlated to effective leadership ability, meaning the smarter the leader, the more effective and successful that leader would be. This should probably go without saying and be somewhat common sense, but researchers operated with somewhat of an incomplete definition of intelligence. When people first started researching trait theory, this trait was defined only by the level of intellectual ability that one possessed. Therefore, the identification of intelligence as a major leadership factor in the early twentieth century did not come without some unscrupulous implications.

For the most part, the original definition of leadership intelligence coincided with and reflected the popular viewpoint of organizations. In the early twentieth century, organizations were compared to machines. You put something in, and you get something out.

People were looked at as just parts to the machine that kept it running. This gave birth to shallow leadership at every level of society, including the Christian church. Even the most intelligent leaders, both secular and spiritual, had trouble connecting with their followers to foster motivation, creativity, and genuine "buy-in." It was obvious that this shallow definition for intelligence was not sufficient, as intellect alone could not provide the basis for high-level leadership. It was not until the 1990s that researchers began to see intelligence as a deeper phenomenon.

During the 90s, new concepts such as emotional intelligence, social intelligence, and cultural intelligence emerged as a way to describe a leader's level of leadership intelligence along with intellect. Emotional intelligence refers to the ability of a leader to connect with followers by recognizing their emotions, as well as their own, while showing compassion and empathy. Social intelligence is defined as selecting appropriate responses and dealing with situations appropriately considering the social environment. Cultural intelligence is a leader's ability to recognize and discern key elements of different cultures (of societies, civilizations, and even organizations) that may hinder or further an organization's goal. As you can see, the original definition of intelligence falls short because organizations, including the church, are not as simple as machines. They possess very complicated systems and interactions of different people.

Although these definitions are not exhaustive, it gives us a picture as to why simple intellect is not enough to effectively lead. When you lead people, you have to interact with them. You have to motivate them. You have to drive them to be the best that they can be. Simple intellect will not do that. A leader must also possess social, emotional, and cultural intelligence in order to fully connect with followers and to inspire them. Proverbs 4:7 states, "Wisdom is the principal thing; therefore get wisdom: and with all thy getting get understanding." Intelligence is very important, but true understanding comes when you go beyond the surface and sympathize with those you lead through the discernment of emotional, social, and cultural stimuli.

Self-Confidence

Self-confidence is a rather touchy subject when it comes to leadership. You will find that many of the renowned leaders throughout history had a great deal of self-confidence. This was another major trait identified by the "great man" researchers throughout the twentieth century. However, it's a sensitive matter because one must find the proper balance between a healthy level of self-confidence and humility to be a successful leader, especially one in God's ranks.

Humility is a subject that we will discuss in a later chapter, but many have a skewed view of what it really means. Humility is not degrading oneself as a disguise to appear meek and lowly. Such actions are those of pseudo-humility, which is actually a form of pride. Many leaders want to appear to be humble by overly emphasizing their short falls, failures, and inadequacies. Leaders that engage in such activities are often just simply insecure and not necessarily humble.

Even though humility may be more important in spiritual leadership settings, it is still a major trait that leaders in the secular realm must find as well, at least to a degree. Too much self-confidence is, or at least can be interpreted as, pride. However, not enough self-confidence will render a leader helpless when challenging situations arise. A healthy self-confidence level for spiritual leaders comes from knowing who you are in Christ. The popular way to express this is by saying, "I know who and whose I am."

The apostle Paul knew how to display a proper balance. He was confident not in his abilities alone but in his God and his God's ability to use the talents that he possessed. In 2 Corinthians 12, Paul makes it clear that he would rather brag about all of the perils and infirmities that God has brought him through than he would about his own accomplishments! This is godly self-confidence: knowing that we are valuable in the kingdom, but in context and in the grand scheme of things we are nothing without God and His grace! Believe it or not, the kingdom will move forward without you. Some find that to be a troubling thought, but it is true. God will always have a remnant of people from which to draw out leaders to perform His exploits on this earth. We should not find that surprising if we read our Bibles.

Determination

Determination is absolutely essential to successful leadership. Determination is usually described as a willingness to get the job done and includes such characteristics as initiative, perseverance, persistence, and drive. Without these qualities, leaders will fail because they possess no drive to carry them beyond the hard times.

Look, I am not going to sugarcoat it. Leadership in the kingdom of God is hard. Once you decide you are going to follow the will and calling of God, you become a target of the enemy. Satan will do everything in his power to destroy that calling because he is doing everything in his power to destroy God's witness on earth. And do you want to know the worst part about it? God will let him do it — at least to some degree! That might be a hard pill to swallow, but it is true. A former pastor of mine, once told me that God would not use someone greatly until he allows them to be hurt deeply! Why do we find this hard to believe?

The apostle Peter declares, "Beloved, think it not strange concerning the fiery trial which is to try you, as though some strange thing happened unto you" (1 Peter 4:12). Think about all of the major leaders in the Bible: Abraham, Moses, Joshua, Samuel, David, and the list goes on. They were all completely different leaders with different strengths and weaknesses. Other than the fact that they served God and they were of the same nationality, they only had one thing in common: *they all experienced hard times during the course of their leadership career.* These hard times were designed by God to build character and to mold and shape them into leaders who would align with His will for His people at that particular time.

As a leader in the kingdom of God, you will have to have a made-up mind. You have to be determined to let nothing move you but God! Not famine, not fear, not fame, not anything, save the Lord Jesus Christ. If you want to build trust with others, then you have to show a relentless trust in God because other people will not fully trust you if you cannot trust Him. But rest assured, we can be confident that the words of Philippians 1:6 are true: "he which hath begun a good work in you will perform it until the day of Jesus Christ."

Remember that this statement came from a man that endured hardships everywhere he went. As a matter of fact, he was in prison when he wrote that very statement! Not only was he in prison but also all scholars generally agree that he was being held captive in Rome, where he would latter die as God's martyr! Though he felt that the end was near, he never questioned God. Throughout all of his trials, he never got mad at Him. He used those times to give God glory, and he allowed Him to mold and shape his character. If you are truly called to leadership in the kingdom, you will face some hard times, but you will also receive from God the strength and grace sufficient to overcome and arise as gold that has been tried in the fire of circumstance so that you may reflect His glory more perfectly!

Integrity

Integrity is of utmost importance when discussing the trait theory of leadership. This trait describes one's degree of honesty and trustworthiness. Furthermore, one that clings to a strong set of moral and ethical principles while taking responsibility for every action is described as having integrity. Leaders with integrity are infinitely more effective at casting shared vision and inspiring those they lead to action! This is because integrity fosters trust and commitment. Integrity is the most powerful leadership trait, but it is also the most evasive. In other words, once it is gone it is very hard to get it back.

Is this not *the* leadership trait that is lacking today in many offices of leadership? If there is ever a day when leaders need to be mindful of their actions and have moral and ethical backbone it is now! We live in a world where moral relativism has evolved into a hostile takeover! Murder is justified and disguised as abortion, God's idea of marriage is under satanic attack, and the human body is no longer defined by standards of man and womanhood but by how someone feels at a certain time. And, if you are against these wicked ideas, then you are intolerant and hateful and must be destroyed! That is the world we live in now. They will, as Jesus said, offer you up to be killed! With this in mind, do you still want to lead? You should if you are truly called of God, but you should at least have a healthy understanding of what you will face. God's leaders need moral backbone, which is very much lacking in the traditional secular idea of leadership.

Consider this excerpt taken from Dr. David Abshire's work *Facing the Character Crisis in America*, which describes some figures associated with then popular organizations:

> *Suisse First Boston-1.5; ImClone-7; Rite Aid-8; Enron- 10; Adelphia-20; Dynergy-24.5; WorldCom-25. The stock price of these firms? Perhaps the return or equity? No, those are the numbers of years that senior executives of those firms were sentenced to prison.*

Smart and talented men and women led these organizations. So, what happened? Where did they go wrong? They infringed upon a moral and ethical code that was supposed to act as a beacon and warning system. You can have all the intellect in the world, but that will not protect you from corruption!

I know that this reflects the immorality of a secular business world gone wrong, but the sobering truth is that the same thing can and has happened in spiritual leadership. How many preachers have been found in adultery? How many church secretaries and other members of leadership have embezzled church funds? You think to yourself, "well that was them; I would never do such a thing!" You better wake up and realize that more anointed men and women than us have fallen prey to the enemy's subtlety!

Eroding morals in leadership have created a vicious cycle in both the spiritual and secular world that continues to spiral downward. This downward spiral will undoubtedly continue as evil men and seducers become worse and worse (see 2 Timothy 3:13). However, we have the chance to stand up in the face of this evil and overcome temptation.

A failure in the realm of integrity is really just a failure to serve others. Leaders that have fallen prey to this have turned the focus onto serving themselves instead of ministering to others. It is selfishness at its core and will destroy your leadership, but most importantly it will destroy others in the process! We never stop to realize just how much we affect someone else's walk with God.

Jesus rebuked the Pharisees just about every time he encountered them. They were supposed to be spiritual leaders. People looked up to them and turned to them for guidance. But they were so full of themselves that they had no clue as to the identity of true leadership. In Matthew 23:15 Jesus boldly declares, "Woe unto you, scribes and Pharisees, hypocrites! for ye compass sea and land to make one proselyte, and when he is made, ye make him twofold more the child of hell than yourselves."

Here is the problem. These Pharisees would go out and "lead" people to God. Yea! All right! High fives all around! Another one has been saved! Not so fast! Jesus said that in the process, they made that new convert twice the demon spawn that they were. Add in the compounding effect of soul winning, and the person that this new convert "leads" to Christ may become four times worse than the original.

It was said before that James warns us not to blindly jump into leadership (see James 3:1). We will have to account for every person that we lead astray, maybe not to the degree that a pastor will, but for all intents and purposes we will be held accountable. Don't think for a second that you will get off the hook for leading someone astray! It is important to understand that we will be held accountable for how we lead and what we do with the "talents," minds, and souls that God has entrusted in our hands.

The ultimate question that we have to ask ourselves with all honesty is Would I follow me? I think that if we are honest with ourselves then we would not be so quick to answer, but we would examine ourselves and strive to keep our hearts with all diligence (see Proverbs 4:23; 2 Corinthians 13:5).

Infringe on the boundaries of integrity and you will never get it back, at least not the full extent that it was in the eyes of those that you lead. Yes, you can be forgiven, but there are consequences that you will live with that will continue to haunt you for the rest of your life in some cases. This is because human beings can forgive, but we can't forget. Your family and your congregation will always remember when you committed adultery. Your team members will always remember when you cheated them. Your Sunday school students will always remember when you walked out on them. They may continue to *love* you, but they may never again truly and committedly *follow* you.

Sociability

Finally, the last common trait identified by the "great man" researchers was sociability. Sociability refers to the leader's ability to form meaningful relationships with those they lead as well as their colleagues. It should go without saying that if a leader can't build rapport with people, then eventually he will look over his shoulder and see nobody following behind.

A leader's ability to connect with people is crucial to success, especially in the realm of spiritual leadership. The popular leadership adage is "they won't care how much you know until they know how much you care." For instance, a pastor that has a hard time empathizing with the members of his congregation will find fewer people knocking on his door for spiritual advice and direction. This is because sociability is a powerful prerequisite to leadership influence. If you can't connect with people on a deeper level, then they will not trust you. And if they can't trust you, then you most certainly can't lead them. It is as simple, and as complicated, as that.

A key principle to remember here is to slow down. Many times, leaders are so busy that they forget about the present moment. Walk slowly through the crowd so that you can make yourself available to those hurting in the present. Jesus himself commanded us to be available to those we lead. This principle is especially evident in the parable of the Good Samaritan (see Luke 10). The leaders (a priest and a Levite) that passed by the wounded man had an opportunity to minister to him that they would never have again. We should never be too busy to help someone in need. Of course, this comes with an ability to truly connect with those you lead.

The good news is that those aspiring to leadership can learn all of these traits, at least to a degree that they can be successful. For example, I was not born a social person. In fact, I was probably the biggest introvert that I ever met. However, through time I allowed God to change my personality. As I heard Him call me to leadership, I allowed myself to be put on the Potter's wheel. And, you can do the same.

❧

Closing and Transition

While the entire first chapter of this book was spent expounding on some key points of the history of leadership thought, the remaining chapters will deal with the true identity and source of power for spiritual leaders. All of the previous content is good scholarship and information that will make your leadership better and prepare you for God's calling. However, it is not *the* principle and most important aspect with which you should be concerned.

Although a potential leader can learn enough to be "dangerous" in the leadership realm, it will not and cannot suffice as *the* direction from which comes your promotion and ascension to spiritual leadership. God's chosen leader must be anointed. And while you can learn how to feel after the Spirit of God, you cannot "learn" anointing. Such things are poured out on those that God chooses. This anointing can come from no other place or direction than from Him directly.

Chapter Two

David: The Model for Godly Promotion

"For promotion cometh neither from the east, nor from the west, nor from the south. But God is the judge: he putteth down one, and setteth up another"
— PSALM 75:6-7

Although Psalm 75 is attributed to Asaph, it directly points to and describes the circumstances surrounding how David came to claim the throne. In fact, many scholars actually believe that Asaph, via public speech or otherwise, received these words directly from king David himself and disseminated them among the kingdom. Certainly, it would make perfect sense in regard to how eloquently this definition of leadership was penned. No one knew the importance of and truth of God's promotion more than David. He waited many years after he was anointed by Samuel to claim the kingdom.

Sadly, I think most would-be leaders grow weary of waiting only a small fraction of this time especially in a day and age where attention spans are at a minimum. But David not only waited for God's promotion, he understood the power of allowing God's timing and purpose to come to fruition. He could have taken the throne at any time during that lengthy period. He had the strength, wisdom, courage, and anointing not only to take the throne, but maybe even march crusader style into the capital itself and forcefully rip it away from Saul.

Some may say it was his right and spiritual duty to do so. However, I say for him not to do so was an act of worship and reverence to God who promotes at His own time and will.

 exo

While You Wait
Throughout David's waiting period, we find many obstacles that would have succeeded in destroying

his leadership had he folded and given up. If it wasn't Saul trying to kill him, it was Nabal refusing to give him provision. If it wasn't Nabal, then it was the Amalekites at Ziklag who destroyed his village and took away the wives of both him and his men.

If would-be leaders are not careful, they can get caught in the rat race of trying to reach some position and wind up getting bitter and frustrated because it hasn't happened in their time. This is the way of the world not God. He says that promotion comes from Him. The world, its ways, and its system are tools in the hand of the Almighty for one purpose: to bring about His will.

Since we live in a world that places priority on position, however, we are faced with a challenge. We can allow ourselves to get destroyed by all of the obstacles in between us and our rightful place in the kingdom of God, or we can choose to overcome. The leadership lessons that we can learn from the events prior to David's reign are powerful.

Temptation to Usurp Authority
No examples point to David's loyalty and willingness to wait on God more than what we read in 1 Samuel.

The first example is in chapter 24. Saul is sleeping in a cave with an army of three thousand men. David sneaks into the camp (he was already hiding in the same cave as Saul) and gently cuts off the bottom of Saul's robe. There are many principles to expound here that pertain to the topic of leadership but none more important than loyalty. In keeping with our premise of waiting for God's promotion, we find that David could have ended Saul's reign right then and there, but he refused to touch God's anointed. Notice that David had a reverence and under-standing of spiritual authority. One does not have a right to usurp authority just because the powers that be may not be spiritually healthy.

Notice how David reacted to what he did. The Bible says that his "heart smote him" (v. 5) just because he cut off part of Saul's garment.

David had a true servant's heart. Years before this, he went to battle with a giant all because king Saul was too scared to do his spiritual and kingly duty to defend Israel. No one matched up more pound-for-pound with Goliath than Saul, as he stood head and shoulders above every other man in Israel. If anyone should have fought Goliath, it should have been Saul. But no, he left it to a shepherd boy, a little shepherd boy with a big heart and great faith in his God. After this, David played the harp in the presence of king Saul to cheer him up. He served God's anointed. He loved God's anointed.

And so, this servant's heart smote him because he cut off the skirt of the anointed. Why did he pick the skirt of the garment? It was probably because it was the easiest to cut off without getting caught, but I have another thought. Whether David realized it at the time or not, this was actually a symbol of the tearing away of the bond between Saul and himself.

In the Old Testament, men used the skirts of their robes to mark their approval and acceptance. Boaz spread the skirt of his robe over Ruth as a symbol of accepting her and his responsibility as the kinsmen redeemer (see Ruth 3:9). In like manner, God spoke through Ezekiel, signifying His acceptance of Israel using this same image (see Ezekiel 16:8). When Jesus cried out to Jerusalem and noted that he had desired to cover it in the shadow of his wings, he used this same analogy as the Hebrew word for "skirt" could be translated as "wings" (see Luke 13:34). Even though the New Testament was written in a different language than the Old Testament, Jesus was well aware of Jewish customs and metaphors.

Therefore, we see that David may have used this as an example to show Saul that they used to be bound together in love. They used to have a special relationship built on loyalty and trust. He even called Saul "father," which was a very intimate word in the Hebrew language. Now, that bond was severed because of Saul's desire to kill him.

The second example, found in chapter 26, shows another poignant example of David's loyalty and desire for Saul to come to his senses. Once again, we find Saul asleep, symbolic of his being asleep spiritually. This time David and Abishai, his nephew and one of his generals, went down to the camp after a deep sleep from the Lord had fallen upon Saul and his men. Once there, David held Abishai back from killing Saul and said:

"As the LORD liveth, the LORD shall smite him; or his day shall come to die; or he shall descend into battle, and perish. The LORD forbid that I should stretch forth mine hand against the LORD's anointed" (1 Samuel 26:10-11).

Again, David refused to harm Saul because of the reverence that he had toward God and His anointed. He did, however, take Saul's spear and a cruse of water from his side. Why did he take these things? Again, he wanted evidence to show Saul that he was there. But, just like the last time, there is some symbolism involving the items that David took. First, he took Saul's spear. This was most likely the same javelin that Saul threw at David multiple times while he played music in the king's court. Maybe David took this javelin and showed it to Saul hoping that it would remind him of the evil that Saul had in his heart.

He also took Saul's cruse of water. Since water is a pure substance, maybe David chose this item because it symbolized a pure and honest vessel. Maybe by taking it from Saul he hoped to show the king that he was not acting honorably and purely.

When Saul awoke, David showed him that he could have killed him again but did not. He showed him the spear and the cruse of water. Notice also that David gave the spear back, but he kept the vessel. Whether David knew it at the time or not, this was a symbol that God had stripped the kingdom from a man that once had a pure heart and given it to the man after God's own heart, which by definition is pure, but also holy, just, and merciful (1 Samuel 10:6-9; 1 Samuel 13:14). And, if we are going to be after His heart, then we must trust that He is who He says He is.

In all of this, even though he never hurt a hair on the king's head, his heart smote him. He felt guilt and shame for even putting himself in a position to hurt God's anointed. David's heart still hurt because even though he may have been born and anointed to lead, he desired and longed to first serve.

That's why we have to be careful what we allow ourselves to be around and to whom or what we join ourselves. You can cause some serious damage by just being in the presence of people that talk negatively about your pastor. There are also other ways that you can put yourself in a position to "kill" the Lord's anointed.

I have seen charismatic leaders come into a church and steal the hearts of the people away from the pastor. This is tragic, and it is not in any way, shape, or form part of true spiritual leadership. Such people are power mongers, seeking only the gratification of their self-elevated egos. They are not fit for kingdom leadership. Yet, many are led astray. You can even do this subconsciously to a certain extent. Always be mindful of your position and stance physically, psychologically, and spiritually because you could be putting yourself in a position conducive to spiritual murder!

Temptation of Distraction
Another leadership lesson is found in David's dealings with Nabal (see 1 Samuel 25). David protected Nabal's servants in Carmel. In return, he asked Nabal for some of his provision. Seeing that Nabal was a very wealthy man, he had plenty to spare.

However, Nabal refused and berated David's men. Then David, in his frustration, gathered his men to get ready to take everything Nabal had and burn his place to the ground. However, God sent a voice through Abigail to stop him. And the Lord ended up fighting that battle, so David wouldn't have to deal with it. Now, there are some interesting insights here.

First, Nabal's name means "fool." Leaders, especially in the church, have to deal with all kinds of different people, and they occasionally stumble upon these types of situations. The Bible instructs us to call no one a fool (which actually means that you have written them off as hopeless), but there are foolish people, and foolish people do foolish things.

Sometimes these things are huge matters that need to be dealt with immediately as David had purposed. However, leaders can focus all their attention on the minority of fools and foolish behavior that they neglect to see more pressing matters and/or the bigger picture.

If David had carried out what he had purposed to do to Nabal's household, then Abigail would have surely died in the crossfire. Interestingly enough, if David did not hearken to the voice that God sent him, he surely would have been in danger. The Bible says that Nabal lived in Maon, which was located just eight miles south of Hebron. The problem with that is Saul had heard about David's whereabouts and quickly pursued him.

If David would have made his way northward from the wilderness of Paran to Maon, then he would have been that much closer to Saul and his army as they traveled south to Ziph! See, chasing fools will likely get you in trouble. Leave them alone; don't waste your time with them. God will deal with them and the issue. Don't put yourself or your ministry in danger on account of a Nabal!

The second thing to understand is that God puts voices in your life. These voices come in many forms. They may be fellow ministers, it may be your spouse, and even the Holy Ghost in you is a voice. God uses these voices to lead and guide you while you are in the wilderness so to speak. Learn to listen to those voices. Value their advice and direction as David valued that of Abigail, and it will surely save your ministry, and at the same time have a lasting effect on your spiritual prosperity.

Temptation to Fold

The last account of David's obstacles that we will discuss is the tragedy at Ziklag. David and his six hundred men, all with families, lived in Ziklag, which was a city given to David by the king of Gath of the Philistines while he pretended to be in allegiance to him (see 1 Samuel 27:6). When they came back from meeting with the lords of the Philistines, they found that the Amalekites had burned their homes to the ground and taken their wives captive. David subsequently invaded the land of the Amalekites and took back what was taken from them.

As we encounter a rather dark scenario in David's life, there are some more invaluable leadership lessons. The first is that you, as a leader or leader in waiting, will experience setbacks; attacks from the enemy that will destroy you and your ministry if you let them. The enemy will come in and try to lay claim on the promises that God has given to you. When that happens, you need to do what David did: encourage yourself in the Lord!

We have heard it preached up and down this very principle, but what I often do not hear a preacher say is what David did after he encouraged himself. It is going to take a lot more than a pep talk with the Lord. Don't misunderstand me. Prayer is vital, prayer is pivotal, and prayer is paramount. If we do not have a quality prayer life then we are leading and being led of the flesh, not the Spirit. So prayer is needed first and foremost. But, too many times people just stop at the prayer. Once you have prayed and encouraged yourself you need to take action! David marched into enemy territory and took back what the enemy had stolen from him!

Has the enemy taken your joy, peace, love, or interest that you once had in the ministry? Pray, encourage yourself in the Lord, and take it back with Holy Ghost authority! Perhaps God allowed that old devil to take it from you in order to light a fire under your spiritual behind. Rise up my friend and take it back! God has got a plan for you. He has got a ministry for you. Don't let the enemy claim what is rightfully yours; take it back! Don't let setbacks like these ruin what God has beautifully designed for you.

Now, let's take a look at this enemy who attacked Ziklag. An interesting concept is uncovered when you start to investigate the identity of these Amalekites. First of all, they were the ones that snuck up behind the children of Israel during their exodus from Egypt and killed all that lagged behind: the old, feeble, injured, and defenseless. That is the tactic of the enemy. He will kick you when you are down. But we must not let him keep us down. Furthermore, God vowed to destroy the Amalekites from the face of the earth (see Exodus 17:14). This task fell to Saul when God, through the prophet Samuel, commanded that he go and utterly destroy the Amalekites and everything that pertained to them (see 1 Samuel 15).

However, we know that Saul failed this mission and left some alive. When we fast-forward several years, we find that the very same thing that David's leader, king Saul, was supposed to protect him from has now attacked him! David could have easily blamed the leadership. He could have placed blame publicly on Saul for this tragedy, but he didn't. He had too much respect for God's anointed!

It doesn't matter what you think the leadership over you should or shouldn't do. You have no right to discredit or sow discord. Let God be God and continue to do what is right and honorable. God will make good on His promises toward you, and then, once you are in the position or one like it, you can see how "easy" it is to be *the* leader and make decisions. Not that Saul has an excuse here, as his decisions fall on the immoral side of leadership behavior. He needed someone to come to him and talk to him about it. But too many times people criticize the general decisions of God's anointed when they don't even know all of the facts. In simple terms, stay out of God's Kool-Aid if you don't know the flavor! And, even if you do, then keep it to yourself. If it bothers you that much, then tell God about it, and let Him tell you to stay out of it. Obviously, the principle of not getting involved does not apply to immoral acts and decisions. Pray for your leaders that they don't fall into gross temptations. Let us not forget that the very thing that Saul neglected

to destroy came back and destroyed him in the end
(see 2 Samuel 1:8).

cxo

Final Thoughts and Transition

From these examples, we can gather that David's
waiting period is a good model for aspiring spiritual
leaders. Notice that the fact he had not yet received
the promise did not keep him from performing some
of the very actions that accompany the monarchy!
It didn't take long for people to recognize the
anointing. In the beginning, four hundred men came
to him, and he led them with integrity, purity, and
nobility (see 1 Samuel 22:1-2). The very next chapter
ascribes six hundred men in his band (see 1 Samuel
23:13). You see, leadership is not about position,
it's about action! Slay some "giants" and people
will recognize the calling. Save some "cities" from
eminent death and more will seek your counsel.

The point is that David led—even when he
waited to lead. You can be a leader in whatever
capacity you are in right now. Don't wait for God
to give you that position to start leading; lead now!
Lead in worship among the congregation, lead in

prayer, lead in your youth group, lead in teaching Bible studies, lead by example.

It didn't matter where David found himself; he made sure that he was practicing his leadership. While he waited, he learned how to be patient, he learned how to trust in God, he learned how to escape the enemy's grasp, and he learned how to fight for what God had promised him. And he did all of this as a valiant leader with confidence in God and the gifts and talents that God had given him.

We expounded some of the events that surrounded David's eventual ascension to the throne to show a model for all would-be spiritual leaders. That model is servanthood. Even though he may not have agreed with everything his leader did or said, he remained loyal to God's anointed and ultimately to God. Even though he was truly anointed of God for the position, he would not under any circumstances do anything to forcefully bring about God's will. He understood spiritual authority and how to wait upon God for promotion

The ultimate lesson to learn here is that God's timing is impeccable! He allows us to go through periods of waiting and obstacles for a purpose. He may have anointed you to do some great work for the kingdom, but that doesn't mean that you are ready to accept the responsibility that comes along with it.

The anointing happens before the crowning in order to grow our confidence in God, so we have something to stand on when times get rough. When we feel as though God is not holding up His end of the bargain, just remember that he is "not slack concerning his promise" (2 Peter 3:9). What God has said, He will perform. He gives us the anointing to carry us through the hard times while we learn and grow into the measure and stature of the person that He wants us to be *before* we take that promised position.

Now that we understand that promotion comes only from God, we can begin to scrutinize all the other modes and avenues that people use to try to get ahead. We find many of these ulterior motives and concerns right here in Psalm 75:6-7. As spiritual leaders and spiritual leaders-in-waiting, it is important to understand wrong motives come in many different shapes and forms. Leadership thought and theory contains principles of the different uses of power, which are really just different ways of influencing people. Leaders will attempt, whether consciously or subconsciously, to use five different forms of power: expert power, coercive power, referent power, reward power, and legitimate power. Each one carries with it certain fallacies and consequences in spiritual leadership if motivated by the flesh and trusted in apart from God. However, the same can be honed and used for the glory of God as well.

Therefore, the remainder of this book is dedicated to exposing the danger of trusting in these forms of power without the guidance and unction of the Holy Ghost.

Chapter Three

Promotion from the East: Expert Power and Intellect

"I am not a natural leader.
I'm too intellectual;
I'm too abstract; I think too much."
— NEWT GINGRICH

Many leaders, and spiritual leaders at that, fail because they trust that their intellect alone is enough to get them to where they think God wants them to be. They become so vested in vision through the fleshly human mind that they become blind to the things in the spiritual realm. Although touched on as an essential leadership trait in the first chapter, what follows are more specific points regarding trusting solely in your own intellect.

Certainly, the kingdom of God needs intellectual men and women to rise up to positions of leadership, especially in a day and age where so much stock is placed in education. But the fallacy here is that many trust solely or too much in intellect and fail to see God's plans. Such leaders walk by sight not by faith. Such leaders completely miss out on the true identity of leadership and its implications for God's people. After all, when God decided to robe Himself in flesh and dwell among us, He did not call the renowned experts, doctors, and lawyers of the Law to follow him. He called a bunch of unlearned fishermen and a hated tax collector.

Granted, these men were extremely knowledgeable in their own craft and vocation, but not so much in the realm in which God called to walk. Does that make them unfit for leadership simply because they didn't have the same "knowledge" as the more learned individuals of their day. No, absolutely not! In fact, this made them perfect for God's work because their minds had not yet been tainted and filled with all kinds of misconceptions, heresies, and vain traditions of man as those "more refined" folk.

Sure, they had their own issues and misconceptions about what spiritual leadership is, but Jesus took every opportunity to properly instruct them differently. And, because they were not so full of themselves (except for Judas), they were pliable. God made them who He wanted them to be because they were not already what they wanted themselves to be. So, let's keep everything in perspective, shall we?

Proverbs 3:5-8 states:

Trust in the LORD with all thine heart; and lean not unto thine own understanding. In all thy ways acknowledge him, and he shall direct thy paths. Be not wise in thine own eyes: fear the LORD, and depart from evil. It shall be health to thy navel, and marrow to thy bones"

It is interesting to see here that God equates trusting in our own understanding to evil. This is because the carnal mind is dangerous and can lead many astray. The leader himself can fall to the lies of prosperity that intellect alone says that it can provide.

Think about this: Samson did not fall because of his arrogance or the loss of his strength alone. These were only symptoms of a much bigger problem: He thought that he could outsmart everyone else! It didn't work with the men he told the riddle to in Judges 14, and it didn't work when he was faced with a vexing and inquisitive woman with whom he had no business being anyway.

He thought that he could handle it, and that was the biggest lie of them all. He thought he was smarter than everyone else, and he thought wrong. Many fall into this line of thinking, as it is one of the most common leadership fallacies in today's society. Let's look deeper at its significance to leadership.

~

Significance of the East

Psalm 75:6-7 notes that the source of promotion, or leadership, does not come from the geographical location of the East. For centuries, the Eastern hemisphere has represented wisdom and intellect. Many of the greatest minds have come from the Eastern countries of the world. That is because they place a high value on intelligence and education is woven into their culture as part of achieving social status. A focus on intellect directly lines up with the leadership principle of expert power.

တော

Expert Power Defined

Expert power is when leaders can get people to follow them simply because of their wide knowledge base, their intellect gained from education and experience. People often respect and acknowledge those who have taken the time to invest in their own education. Similarly, people with a lot of experience in certain matters are sought after for advice and counsel in their field of expertise.

The use of expert power is not the problem; it's the abuse of expert power that gets people in trouble. Placing too much emphasis on it will drive a wedge between you and God simply because it sends the message: "I am good God; I don't need your advice anymore." I certainly hope that none of us would actually come out and say that to God, but doesn't He already know our hearts better than we do? This is what we implicitly say to Him when we desire knowledge more than Him. We should not be concerned so much with the word or knowledge of this world that it takes priority over the Word of God. Set your priorities in order and watch God give you the experience, wisdom, and knowledge necessary to lead His people closer to Him. There is a godly way to use this power.

Expert power can be very useful especially in the kingdom of God. Every leader in the church can use their expert power to glorify God and edify the church. For example, a major part of leadership is training others how to do certain things. This is the crux of leadership: making other leaders.

A lead usher will have to train others on such things as how to greet, how to direct parking, where to seat guests, and the order of taking up an offering. Similarly, a Bible study teacher needs to under-stand the plan of salvation. He would also need a very good grasp of the biblical narrative and how the two covenants (both Old and New Testaments) work together to form the complete masterpiece of God. If these leaders in the church lack the necessary knowledge to train others, then their expert power is nil. If a leader has little to no expert power, then their chances of being called upon by God or their pastor to actually lead is greatly diminished.

This is a foundational biblical principle. The apostle Paul admonishes us to "Study to shew thyself approved unto God, a workman that needeth not to be ashamed, rightly dividing the word of truth" (2 Timothy 2:15). This is a well-known verse, and one that we in Pentecost often use. We use it to show the importance of studying the Bible and understanding God's Word. However, Paul is actually using an analogy. The word *workman* here comes from the Greek word *ergates*, which means "an actual laborer for hire." The fact of the matter is, no master would hire anyone to do anything if they didn't know what they are doing. Whether they are pastors, ushers, Sunday school teachers, or music ministers is immaterial. The principle is this: you better have some expert power. Our level of stewardship concerning the things of God as well as the physical logistics of the office in which we serve characterizes this.

Timothy's field of work was pastoring. So, very fittingly, Paul tells him that he better not find himself ashamed because he doesn't know his work backward and forward. If someone were to come to Timothy and ask about salvation, could he have eloquently expounded the scriptures that it would motivate people to conversion? This was the question of which Paul was concerned. He was telling Timothy that he had better know his craft. The importance of knowing the Word of God is vital for everyone in the house of God from the pastor to the one that is seemingly not interested in working in the church. However, every leader, whether Sunday school teacher, college and career director, or youth leader, can even find themselves ashamed if they don't know the other specifics of their own office!

It is vital that Sunday school teachers learn how to effectively communicate the Word of God to children. In the same vein, it is paramount for youth leaders to understand the struggles that teens face in this present day. If leaders fail to have expert power in the spiritual vocation in which God has placed them, then they will lack the type of influence that they need to inspire people to grow in Christ! Expert power is a valid form of leadership power, but the fallacy lies in the fact that many place sole priority on it and push God out of the equation.

❧

Biblical and Historical Examples

History is riddled with success stories and failures that relate to how leaders regarded their own intellect. Those who placed sole priority on their own intellect and abilities fell and fell hard. On the other hand, those that recognized the source of intellect and power rose up to do great things and were directed of God. Let's explore some of these examples.

Daniel and the Chaldeans

The early Mesopotamians were famous for their intellect. Historical evidence is found in the fact that this region formed the very first civilizations and writing systems. Later, king Hammurabi assembled a vast compilation of legal decisions forming the very first judicial library and a very explicit source of historical information. Eventually, through some political maneuvering and warfare, this group became the Chaldeans that we know from the Bible. Much is said about these Chaldeans. Most of it reflects upon the priority that they placed on their own intellect.

Daniel dealt directly with the intellect of the Chaldeans. He was captured as a boy from Judah and carried away to Babylon in the first deportation around 605 BC. We find his determination to remain separated from the heathen culture by refusing to partake of the king's meat in Daniel chapter 1. Daniel did this for several reasons, but most notably he knew that the king's meat had been offered to their idol gods, and/or it was taken from unclean animals. He was not interested in such spiritually vile sustenance but chose rather to remain pure and undefiled before God.

It was from this point that God blessed him with supernatural wisdom to combat the intellect of the Chaldeans. He was already smart, but God allowed his gift to grow because he had his priorities in the right place (see Psalm 75:6-7 and Proverbs 18:15-16).

You see, the world has its own wisdom. They will tell you that they have it all figured out. They will try to convince you to give up your "religion" because it's faulty. They will tell you that in order to be "open-minded" and "free thinking" you must rid yourself of the bondage of fables, as they call them. However, what they do not realize is that they are being used as the voice of the Chaldeans just as in Daniel's day. Additionally, they are actually in bondage to the lie that they are "free thinking." The fact of the matter is that the ones claiming freedom and open-mindedness by rejecting God are themselves more influenced by Hollywood, pop-culture, and world events than they would care to admit. If that is the definition of "free thinking," then I would rather be a slave to Christ than have the pseudo-freedom of the world. Someone once said, "I am a fool for Christ. Whose fool are you?"

Daniel went on to interpret dreams and become the head of all those "free thinkers" in Babylon! Don't let the world tell you that in order to get ahead, you must abandon the idea that God will direct your paths. Don't let people lie to you and say that real wisdom comes from science and the like, which is actually just so-called intellectualism (see Colossians 2:8 and 1 Timothy 6:20).

You will be tempted to follow after the way of the world. If you see people doing questionable things, you should not even so much as get close enough to see what is going on. Run from it and run fast! Separate yourself from the world, even if it means to a greater degree than what you see your peers in the church committing to, and God will bless you for it.

In Daniel chapter 5 we see this very example of spiritual leadership excellence. The king of Babylon made a great feast, an ungodly party. They used the gold and silver vessels that they stole from the temple of God in Jerusalem to drink their wine and perform their ungodly acts. How vile, how obnoxious! Belshazzar mocked God just like the world mocks us when we proclaim the truths of the Lord. They tell us we are archaic, foolish, and legalistic, but in reality, we just know where the line has to be drawn.

In the middle of this ungodliness, a hand appeared out of nowhere and wrote on the wall something like this: "You have been weighed in the balances and found to be lacking. Therefore, your kingdom will be given to the Medes and Persians" (paraphrase of Daniel 5:26-28). I find it interesting that none of the king's wise and intellectual men were able to read the writing on the wall. That is because a carnal mind cannot comprehend spiritual things, and neither can it allow itself to be subject to them (see Romans 8:6-7 and 1 Corinthians 2:13-16).

If only the world could see that their ways are folly! If only they could understand the wages of sin is death! But sadly, just like king Belshazzar and his intellectuals, they just can't read the writing on the wall.

Another powerful leadership point in this story is that they had to go find Daniel so that he could read the writing! Although he was the ruler of all the wise men in Babylon and considered a prince, he wasn't at the party. He was not in the room when it happened because he separated himself from ungodliness and self-exaltation. He refused to take part in it just like he refused to eat the king's meat years before he was in position in the king's court! Real leaders don't compromise their morals and values just because they have "arrived." They stay the course that God has established that they may lead people honorably and intellectually as they rely on the Holy Ghost not on their own understanding.

Not only was Daniel separated from the ungodliness, he apparently separated himself from the company of all the other wise men of Babylon. If he had joined himself to them, then he most certainly would have come with them when they came to interpret the writing in the first place. If he had defined and recognized his intellect the same way as the Chaldeans, then he surely would have been there. But no, he did not equate the source of his intellect with the source of their intellect because he recognized that promotion does not come from putting your trust in intellectualism. It comes from God alone! He sets up and tears down whom He wills according to His own good pleasure!

Solomon and the Digression

King Solomon is probably the epitome of wisdom in the Bible. Save the Lord, he is the wisest and smartest man that had ever lived. Was he born that way? No, God made him that way because his heart was in the right place in the beginning. In the beginning, Solomon's desire was not for riches, longevity, or fame. It was to have the wisdom necessary to effectively lead God's people in the way of righteousness (see 1 Kings 3). When we have a pure heart before God, he recognizes it and blesses us accordingly.

King Solomon ruled with the intellect that God gave him for years, and he prospered because of it. Under Solomon's rule, Israel had peace on every side (a feat that would never again be duplicated). However, there came a time when Solomon began to trust in his own wisdom more than the actual source of the wisdom.

The Bible is an amazing masterpiece. Many things that we read seem to make no sense at the time we read them only for the light bulb to go off while reading a completely different book that was written hundreds of years earlier than the first passage. For instance, God laid down certain guidelines for kings long before they made Samuel anoint one (see Deuteronomy 17:14-20). Samuel even warned the people, that the king would do things that they wouldn't like (see 1 Samuel 8:11-18). Now, both Saul and David were guilty of transgressing some of these things, but Solomon blatantly transgressed in every point!

God said that the king should not have many wives (see Deuteronomy 17:17). Well, Solomon had seven hundred wives and three hundred concubines! God said that the king should not seek riches (see Deuteronomy 17:17). Well, Solomon was the richest man on earth. Although the Bible records Solomon as initially being so humble that he refused to ask God for riches, there is no telling where his heart ended up. Even though God had blessed him in that manner, we don't see anywhere in scripture where he dispersed it and blessed others with his wealth. It could be he only heaped it unto himself.

Moving on, God even said that the king should not "multiply horses to himself, nor cause the people to return to Egypt, to the end that he should multiply horses" (Deuteronomy 17:16). Well, not only did Solomon heap to himself multitudes of horses (he had four thousand stalls of them), but he also imported them from . . . wait for it . . . Egypt (see 1 Kings 10:28 and 2 Chronicles 9:28). He failed in every single point!

Much speculation can be made as to why this happened, and we have to understand that he probably didn't have the guidelines written by Moses readily available to him as we do today. However, one has to think that had he not been so consumed with his own wisdom, intellect, and splendor maybe he could have been led of God rather than led astray. See, that's what happens when we let our fleshly desires lead us. We transgress commands that we should know but are oblivious to because we are wise in our own conceit.

Solomon's end was anything but glorious. Though he began as an intellectual for God, he died a fool following after idols. During his digression, he wrote one of the most depressing pieces of literature ever recorded. Although we regard the book of Ecclesiastes as part of the infallible Word of God, and rightfully so, one can tell that it was written by a man who was defeated, depressed, and anything but glorious and victorious.

That's what happens when leaders misplace their priorities and put their trust in their own intellect and understanding. They simply fizzle out. God is not concerned about degrees or pedigrees. He cares about your heart, which is the seat of your motives and intentions. Sadly though, many leaders are only concerned about how to use their intellect to get ahead. Even pastors lose sleep over how to maneuver, position, and grow their church so others will recognize their accomplishments. That is how world leaders use the intellect with which the Almighty has graciously blessed them (yes, they are smart because God gave them the intellect in the first place). However, these things shouldn't be in the kingdom of God.

ॐ

Postmodern Leadership Philosophy

Rene Descartes is widely regarded as the father of modern Western Philosophy and postmodern thought. Many don't know his name, but they can quote his most famous declaration. Descartes wrestled with questions dealing with our existence, and in the end this is what he came up with: "I think, therefore I am". Although he may not have meant to, one cannot really tell, he opened the door for some of the most blasphemous thoughts that had ever raced across the human mind.

Postmodern thought has taken this philosophy to another level by placing absolute authority on a person's intellect and consciousness. The problem with this is that it creates a philosophy that mankind is self-sustaining and absolute. In the postmodern mind, mankind has no need of a God because we can think and act for ourselves using our own intelligence and consciousness.

Now, standing in the twenty-first century, we can see the effects of such thinking. Postmodernism has opened the door to relativism. Relativism, because everyone is right at all times, has paved the way for all sorts of ungodliness (the kind found in 2 Timothy 3:1-9). In the year 2019, we actually have men wanting to be women and women wanting to be men. But not only that, these so-called intellectuals now claim that such "choices" are deserving of the kind of rights that should be reserved for actual genders, races, and ethnicities.

The fact of the matter is that centuries of this "I think, therefore I am" attitude has elevated mankind above their creator (only in their mind, not in reality). Now, the leaders of this day are men and women who have been taught this folly under the guise of being loving and all inclusive.

Now, before you take me out of context, I'm all for human rights and standing up for freedom for all. However, the liberal mind has taken what was a good thing and has perverted it (literally) by extending the basic rights of life, liberty, and the pursuit of happiness that many people died for over the years, to include the right to go against God's law and creation. God made us man and woman, black and white, young and old, and we all have "certain unalienable rights" as our Constitution says.

However, the liberal mind takes these precious freedoms that were created by God and paid for by blood (chiefly that of Christ but also of those who fought through wars and protests) and gives them to people who *choose* to live a certain way. Forget for a second that the way they choose to live is ungodly. The fact that this happens is a slap in the face to those who fought for the freedoms we enjoy. For example, those brave souls that fought for civil rights to be extended to African-Americans did not choose to be black nor did they ask to be enslaved several centuries! Those people suffered and then did something about it. Those people suffered not for a choice but for an identity. The argument that choice is a foundation for unalienable rights is shallow and repulsive, a discredit and insult to those that truly deserve it.

Today, most of our world leaders, are flimsy figures with no moral and ethical backbone. No, they threw their compass away centuries ago while traveling the long, winding, slippery slope of compromise and ungodliness. This is what a focus on intellect has wrought: A godless society. Let us pray that doesn't happen in the church!

∾

Final Thoughts and Transition

What we have just described is the modern thought process, which has infiltrated every facet of humanity. If we are not careful, then we can find ourselves influenced by these same processes and not even know it. That is why it is important to stay full of the Holy Ghost and understand that the source of true power, wisdom, and authority does not come from the East. It is not found in intellect and intelligence. This is only a tool for God to use that He may establish and strengthen you.

Mankind has come up with all kinds of lofty thoughts that attempt to push God out of the process, but all attempts have failed; we are just fooling ourselves. Isaiah 55:6-11 instructs us of the true pinnacle of intellect and gives us the direction for real success, prosperity that comes from the Lord:

> Seek ye the LORD while he may be found, call ye upon him while he is near: Let the wicked forsake his way, and the unrighteous man his thoughts:
>
> and let him return unto the LORD, and he will have mercy upon him; and to our God, for he will abundantly pardon. For my thoughts are not your thoughts, neither are your ways my ways, saith the LORD. For as the heavens are higher than the earth, so are my ways higher than your ways, and my thoughts than

*your thoughts. For as the rain cometh down,
and the snow from heaven, and returneth not
thither, but watereth the earth, and maketh
it bring forth and bud, that it may give seed
to the sower, and bread to the eater: So shall
my word be that goeth forth out of my mouth:
it shall not return unto me void, but it shall
accomplish that which I please, and it shall
prosper in the thing whereto I sent it.*

True wisdom comes only from God. He is the only
self-sustaining One! Don't look to the East to get
your leadership power. Look only to God that He
may be the source and seat of your wisdom.

Chapter Four

Promotion from the West: Coercive Power and Supremacy

"I came, I saw, I conquered."

— JULIUS CAESAR

J ulius Caesar was one of the most successful military commanders of all time. History tells us that it was Caesar who led his armies across the Rhine River to defeat the powerful Gallic tribes. He also conducted the very first Roman invasion of Britain. Many people, those who only know, or care to know, about his valiant conquests against the barbarians, hold Caesar to be the epitome of leadership. However, investigating his life uncovers some eye-opening lessons about his leadership style.

Julius Caesar acquired his positions of power through manipulation, coercion, and military might, forcefully taking what he thought should belong to him. In his final act of defiance as a military commander, he crossed into Rome with his armed legions (an act that was forbidden and considered treason) and ripped the empire away from his contemporaries. Julius Caesar was a phenomenal military commander, but he was no model leader. Looking through the pages of history, it seems that many men followed him simply because they were afraid of him. Instead of being respected, he was feared, and are we to call this leadership?

Sadly, many in the modern era view leadership in this manner as well. They believe that the only way to influence people into doing what they think is best is to manipulate and coerce. Julius Caesar represents the pinnacle of Western authority. King David wrote about acquiring authority in such manner in Psalm 75:6-7. David recognized that leadership does not equal coercion by stating that its source does not come from the West.

෴

Significance of the West

The Western ideal of leadership is characterized by the premise that a vision can only become reality if it's forcefully and/or manipulatively taken. Julius Caesar is a prime example of this thinking, but history is riddled with similar examples of misguided and deranged leaders. Alexander the Great conquered many more lands than Caesar. In fact, the only reason that he stopped conquering before going into Asia was because his men refused to go. Just centuries ago Napoleon Bonaparte attempted to become a Julius Caesar of sorts, but he died in exile. Likewise, consider notorious figures like Stalin, Hitler, and Kim Jung Un. All of these characters define leadership as a function of supremacy.

Interestingly enough, just like the Eastern nations focus on intellect, Western nations have usually always placed their stock in physical power. Although they had an element of intellect in their societies, they placed more focus on their own strength. Leaders of Western countries historically have been naturally assertive. There is also evidence to suggest that this correlates with a non-compassionate view toward people.

The leadership fallacy of supremacy is a major issue that entangles many would-be leaders especially in the church today. Sure, people are more civilized these days. They don't openly declare war and begin dueling in the middle of the sanctuary. No, it's more sly and subtle than that.

Now, manipulation, coercion, and political maneuvering are done more tastefully as if that makes it morally acceptable. Many put their leadership stock in how skillfully they can "handle" people. However, people are not meant to be "handled" like some tool. People are meant to be led with grace and Holy Ghost authority, which is anything but coercive, threatening, or manipulative even in a mild sense. People in the church are not meant to be under overly assertive leaders whose political maneuvering most closely aligns with the leadership principle of coercive power.

Coercive Power Defined

Believe it or not, every leader has the propensity to exert their authority to the point where it crosses the line into coercion—even those in the church. When leaders explicitly or implicitly deal out punishment and withhold rewards in order to force compliance, they follow the way of the business world. Coercive leadership sounds heartless and despicable, and you might be thinking surly this doesn't happen in church leadership, but you would be surprised as to how often we tend to gravitate toward these actions especially if we let our flesh lead us rather than the Holy Ghost. If we remain filled with the Holy Ghost and pliable in the hands of the Lord, then we will learn what godly leadership looks like and display it naturally.

God will not force anyone to do anything. In fact, He doesn't even try to coerce people by tempting them to do things. James 1:13-14 states,

Let no man say when he is tempted, I am tempted of God: for God cannot be tempted with evil, neither tempteth he any man: But every man is tempted, when he is drawn away of his own lust, and enticed.

God is not in the coercion business, and He does not condone these actions from His leaders.

Sadly, though, I have witnessed God's leaders resort to such actions when dealing with unfavorable situations. Now, I am not advocating that God's leaders have no authority. I absolutely believe in spiritual authority. I believe that spiritual leaders have the God-given authority and position to exercise their God-given power at the right time and place. However, this becomes abuse of power and a shift into coercion when the leader becomes led of the flesh and deals out some form of punishment or deprivation just to prove a point that he thinks should be made. Aren't leaders supposed to be teachers? Aren't they supposed to mentor, nurture, and develop people? There is a time to exercise spiritual authority, and there is a time to take the high road and find another way to "teach."

Paul used his spiritual authority perfectly when he rebuked the Corinthian church for condoning the actions of one of their own involving sexual relations with his father's wife (see 1 Corinthians 5). It was time to exercise his power as an apostle once that man and his church family displayed themselves as being non-contrite and defiant. Again, spiritual authority exercised correctly is a sound biblical principle. The command to do everything "decently and in order" applies to the actions of a leader as well to the lives of individuals.

However, many leaders are puffed up and ride on a high horse. How quickly they forget that God had to knock Paul off of his before he showed him the true direction of the Lord. Just like Paul, who was also called Saul of Tarsus, many of God's leaders today think they are doing a great work for God by leading in a boisterous, condemning, and condescending manner. They use harsh words in the pulpit. They appear standoffish and heady, thinking themselves to be noble and holy. This is not Christ-like leadership.

The Lord said that those in the kingdom wishing to become leaders must be servants of all and make themselves least (see Mark 10:44-45). They must put themselves last, not exert themselves to appear lofty before men. Humility is God's blueprint for spiritual leadership. Once, I heard a minister say that God's definition of humility is power under control. Although this is not necessarily a full definition of humility, it is a very valid point.

Every leader commissioned in the church has a certain amount of power given to them by God and their pastor. How they use that power, great or small, is dictated by the extent to which they have allowed God to mold and shape their humility and meekness. When we lose sight of that, we run the risk of resorting to coercion and manipulation to try and drive change and progress.

∽

Biblical and Historical Examples

There are many biblical and historical examples that deal with leaders using coercive power. More often than not, these leaders used them out of place, and it cost them dearly. However, as stated above, there is a time and place where exerting spiritual authority is needed and biblically mandated. In the examples that follow, we find two different scenarios involving the use of coercive power.

Rehoboam and the Intimidation

Following the reign of Solomon, his son Rehoboam inherited an extremely peaceful and prosperous kingdom. In fact, Rehoboam's ensuing decisions after taking the thrown plunged God's people into constant warring and unrest. At the time that Rehoboam claimed the throne, the people were burned out. They had grown weary of the work Solomon had put on them in the building the magnificent temple of the Lord and his extravagant palaces. Rehoboam decided that the wise advice of his father's counselors in making their work easier was not the right direction for the kingdom. Therefore, he listened to his friends' advice to increase the people's workload instead of making it lighter, and he communicated this decision to the people in an unrelenting and condescending fashion. This caused the kingdom to split into two different countries with two different kings, and ultimately two different definitions of spirituality, although both would serve idols at some point.

As a result of Rehoboam's coercive behavior, Jeroboam, one of Solomon's servants who was waiting for the right opportunity to seize the kingdom, convinced all the tribes of Israel except for Judah to follow him. In the end though, their new leader made them worship idols. He completely separated the new kingdom from God, and the people let him because they were bitter and hurt by their former leader's actions. There are numerous lessons and implications in the story of Rehoboam's failed attempt to pound God's people into submission.

First, notice that Rehoboam didn't even give the wise counselors a fair platform to make their case. It appears that Rehoboam was motivated by greed and power. He thought that in order for his kingdom to keep growing, he had to work his people to the bone and make them feel bad when they needed or asked for a break. That sounds cruel doesn't it? You'd be surprised, however, to find that many of God's leaders do the same exact thing.

Many times, a spiritual leader can get so caught up in the desire to grow a church or department that he loses sight of the overall health and wellness, spiritual and physical, of those that he leads. Often, a leader will attempt to coerce and manipulate those who are weary from working themselves to the bone for the kingdom.

Now, I am not advocating to stop prayer meetings, Wednesday night Bible study, or a second service on Sunday. However, I am saying that at some point your people will begin to be overwhelmed by the "work" to the point where it becomes grievous, not rewarding. People get tired, weary, and burned out. At some point a leader is going to have to make a decision between possibly taking a small hit in "growth" because someone wants a break, or they could risk losing families and even souls in the process of exerting his "spiritual authority." If you are a pastor, please remember that people don't have to go to *your* church. If you are a department head, remember that you work with volunteers not slaves. God's leaders need to realize that they are the ones who are blessed by the work of the people not the other way around.

The second issue is that Rehoboam gave no other thought to this problem other than forceful coercion and manipulation. We always look at Rehoboam's wishes for the people to keep working as somehow ungodly. However, it was not the desire for growth that was ungodly, it was the way he attempted to accomplish it. This was his time to be innovative and creative. He could have designed different jobs. He could have created shift work of some kind in order to build rest into the work process. Rather than being the leader that God called him to be,

Rehoboam decided to exert his authority coercively, and it cost him dearly.

Similarly, when faced with logistical dilemmas, leaders in the church have a great opportunity to innovate and create new ministries and processes that make everyone's life and work for God easier, more pleasurable, and more prosperous than ever. Sadly though, the only thing that some leaders know how to do is crack the whip. You will find, though, that when you crack the whip, your members and volunteer staff will respond most likely by finding a crack in the back door and leave your church or department worker-less.

Godly leadership is manifested in love and servanthood not a coercive exertion of authority. Jesus said, "Judge not, that ye be not judged. For with what judgment ye judge, ye shall be judged: and with what measure ye mete, it shall be measured to you again" (Matthew 7:1-2). Treat God's people with dignity and respect, and they will most certainly give back abundantly without feeling like they are being manipulated to do so.

Finally, you never know what will become of the souls that you hurt deeply. Rehoboam lost many people the day he demanded more work from them, but even more devastating than the lost workforce, many ended up losing their souls to idolatry. You see, Rehoboam's actions caused people not only to walk out of his "church," but they also walked out on God. Yes, it is ultimately the decision of the person whether or not to follow God, but don't help them make the wrong decision by being ugly and coercive.

What are we going to say to God when we stand before Him, and He explains to us that someone is in hell partially because of the example we set? And, just because you may not be a pastor, does not get you off of the hook from having to stand before God one day and answer for how badly you treated one of God's little children. Thankfully, we share this responsibility with our pastors who, without question, are ultimately charged with giving an account of everyone they lead. But, regardless of your actual leadership position, you greatly affect those you lead for the good and also the bad. This is dictated largely by how you treat them, and how you genuinely care for their needs while serving them and the kingdom of God.

Let this be a lesson to all leaders, seasoned and aspiring, that promotion is not found in coercion, manipulation, or political maneuvering. It does not come from the West. God decides who leads and who follows based on His sovereign will. If we keep that principle in sight, then God will help us to use the power that He has given us to foster growth in the kingdom as well as personal growth for those we lead.

Josiah and the Cleansing

In 2 Kings 22 we read that Josiah came to rule Judah at only eight years old. However, eighteen years into his reign something happened. He stumbled upon a book, most likely the book of the law of Moses. When he read the law of Moses, he was filled with the fear of the Lord. This fear gave birth to a godly zeal. From that moment on, Josiah sought to utterly destroy all of the high places, graven images, and idolatrous altars in the kingdom. He did this violently at times, but his heart was always in the right place. He desired that the kingdom be a godly nation according to law of Moses.

Isn't this the heart of every true leader of God? I have not met one genuine leader in the church who was not concerned about the spiritual state of God's people. Josiah's zeal can be compared to the zeal of many spiritual leaders. There are some valid leadership lessons to be learned from Josiah and his cleansing of Judah.

First, notice how he was able to bridle his zeal and keep it under subjection. The man was on fire. He sought to burn ungodliness to the ground. He pulled no punches and sought to utterly destroy the works of Satan. Josiah was preaching hell fire and brimstone! But, in the middle of his sermon, he stopped. He noticed a grave off in the distance. Since he was in the process of digging up the bones of the false prophets, he asked who was laid to rest in that particular grave. A man responded that the grave belonged to a prophet of the Lord who actually foretold the exact events surrounding that particular moment in time. This prophet had called Josiah by name and said that he would come one day and rid Judah of ungodliness and idolatry. Josiah instructed to leave that man's sepulcher undisturbed even though there was a false prophet buried in the same grave with him.

By digging up the bones of the false prophets, he essentially exposed ungodliness for what it truly is. That is what spiritual leaders are charged to do: expose ungodliness, dig it up, and destroy it. However, he was able to bridle this zeal and stop short of unnecessary abuse of power when he realized what was at stake in digging up that godly grave.

Would he have been just in digging up the bones of that false prophet that lay in the grave with the man of God? Absolutely, just like every pastor has the God-given right to forcefully expose sin for what it is and preach the truth unapologetically and with no remorse. But Josiah recognized that disturbing a good thing for the sake of forcefully cleansing the land was not what God had in mind. What example would he have set? Where would the line be between good and evil if godliness was handled the same way as ungodliness?

That is the decision every spiritual leader has to make. We must preach unrelentingly against sin. We must proclaim the righteousness of the Lord. But do we crucify people in the process just to prove that point? Absolutely not! God has a way of changing hearts without coercion and ridicule.

I will always remember the words of a wise old minister to a young minister who asked him how to handle people in the church that do things against the Word of God. The old minister replied that in biblical times, a spotless lamb was very hard to come by, but God required one for the atonement of sin. In that time, you essentially had a choice. You could either slaughter all of your spotted lambs and have nothing to offer to God, or you could love those lambs, nurture and feed them, and hope that one day they will give birth to a spotless lamb suitable for sacrifice to God. What powerful words on how to treat difficult people!

Josiah is a perfect example of bridled power that worked toward revival. In addition to burning the graven images, high places, and bones of the false prophets, he also destroyed the houses of the sodomites. This is significant because some would say that the message of the Bible is "God loves everyone the way they are so change is not necessary." Oh, on the contrary. I believe that the true message of the Bible is "God loves everyone the way they are, but He doesn't want to keep them that way"! He loved us while we were sinners, but sinners will not inherit the kingdom of God.

That is why change is necessary. That is why Paul said he "died daily" and put his flesh under subjection (see 1 Corinthians 9:27; 15:31). He also said that if we kill the deeds of the flesh, then we will live (see Romans 8:13). Of course, it is not possible to do this without the Holy Ghost and faith in the work of Christ to reconcile the world.

So, can we really conclude that the message of the Bible is let God love and let sin have its way? That spiritual leaders should just do their best to manage around sin? Absolutely not! Sin is sin and should be dealt with accordingly. Josiah's action against the houses of the sodomites shows every spiritual leader that they don't have to compromise just to appease people.

He absolutely destroyed ungodliness, but he kept his focus squarely on the things that deserved such harshness. Notice that he killed the false prophets on their own altars, he burned down only places of idol worship, and he destroyed only the houses of the sodomites. He kept it in perspective. He hated the sin not the sinner and rebuked the accuser of the brethren not the brethren themselves.

What a powerful example of godly power under control. Using your God-given power like this is sure to earn you respect and foster revival as you help people grow and understand what is acceptable and unacceptable to God.

ഹര

Final Thoughts and Transition

Coercive power can be a deadly force in the kingdom of God. It can eternally wound people if not bridled by the grace and mercy of the Holy Ghost. Many of today's leaders seek to rule with an iron fist. But sadly, they will find that fragile hearts in the hands of those with iron hands results in nothing else but bloodshed and death. Hard hands are unable to mold and shape; they can only pound and flatten. Such leadership is not the way of the godly leader. The source of our promotion should not come from the West. It shouldn't come from coercive power that seeks to manipulate and "handle" people. Our promotion comes from God and God alone who is able to help us bridle our zeal to promote growth not death.

Chapter Five

Promotion from the South: Reward Power and Enticement

"The reward of a thing well done is having done it."
— RALPH WALDO EMERSON

Egypt has long been regarded as a symbol of sin and worldliness in the Bible. The children of Israel were delivered from the bondage of slavery and idol worship much like born-again Christians are when they obey the gospel of Christ. Egypt is also a symbol of great wealth and riches. For centuries, the pharaohs of Egypt lived in splendor and luxury while considering themselves to be gods on the earth. It is interesting to note that Egypt is both a symbol of sin and a symbol of wealth. Perhaps this is because sin and wealth relate so closely together. Jesus said that we couldn't serve both God and money, for the love of money is the foundation and root of all sin (see Luke 16:13; 1 Timothy 6:10).

The correlation of wealth and leadership, though, was so strong in ancient Egypt that the pharaohs were laid to rest in their tombs with all of their riches, thinking that it would accompany them in the afterlife. This is why they built the great pyramids using the slave labor of the less fortunate. They went through great lengths and trouble, for a chance to be able to keep the wealth that they had accumulated over their lifetime. There clearly is a close relationship between sin and wealth and wealth and leadership. We can see how wealth (or the capacity to reward) can be a hinge on a swinging gate. It can be used toward genuine leadership or it can be abused toward sin.

∞

Significance of the South

The regions south of Jerusalem would most closely correlate with what is described as the sub-Saharan and Middle-Eastern societal "clusters". The countries found in the sub-Saharan subculture traditionally tend to stress a high humane-oriented leadership style. That sounds good doesn't it? However, before we think too highly of them, we need to understand something. A humane-oriented leadership style meant that the leader made decisions in order to appease the masses rather than to guide them to growth and development.

The leaders of these countries would tend to use their wealth for the so-called good of the people, but their personal definition of good and what was actually good for the people could be two very different things. This principle doesn't just work with our current subject. No, there are culturally driven principles, ideals, and philosophies that are titled with familiar names and endorsed with a stamp saying, "this is for the good of the people," but they actually have a very different definition and manifestation of that than what we would think. For example, the moniker "freedom of choice" sounds good. However, what they don't tell you is that your choice has to be what they want for you, not necessarily what you actually want.

These types of things are culturally taught; woven and embedded in the very fabric of all societies. As one would expect, this is the source of much cultural conflict around the globe. However, it could also be the source and foundation upon which we can connect with those of different cultures. Truly understanding someone is the basis of genuine relationship building.

The countries found in the sub-Sahara traditionally valued status, which included gathering and accumulating wealth. Now, before we go any further, let me again stress that these observations are not intended to be stereotyping or derogatory in any way but are based on the fully vetted GLOBE study where we find the tendencies, trends, and priorities of countries and cultures all over the world in terms of how they expected leadership to be manifested. (For more on this study, please reference the References and Further Study section at the end of the book.)

We see that status and wealth were high priorities in the areas south of Jerusalem. Therefore the use of what is called reward power was common among leaders in those regions as people greatly desired to be rewarded with riches and honor.

☙✲❧

Reward Power Defined

In simple terms, reward power refers to a leader's ability to influence people through rewarding good behavior as defined by the leader himself. This applies to positive reinforcement, or the actual giving of a gift as a reward to promote compliance. In contrast, coercive power would most likely involve withholding rewards or awards in order to persuade and intimidate. As with the other forms of power, reward power can be used in a good or bad way depending on the leader's focus. If the leader focuses on his ability to reward and uses it as his chief means of influence, then this becomes nothing more than candied manipulation, handling and control that does nothing really to edify the kingdom or bring God glory. Furthermore, using reward power just to get your way will only plant a seed in your heart that most likely will grow into an uncontrollable vine, wrap itself around your leadership goals and then choke the life out of them.

You may think, "Really, is it that serious?." Sure it is. Let's take a look at the leader himself. If he rewards people as a way to get them to do something, doesn't that take the joy and blessing away since their reward is on earth and not in heaven? Scripture states, "Every man according as he purposeth in his heart, so let him give; not grudgingly, or of necessity: for God loveth a cheerful giver" (2 Corinthians 9:7). Manipulating people to give is anything but cheerful, and it will blacken your soul.

Are we in danger of this behavior? Yes, absolutely! Have you ever felt as though you are being pressured by some people to rapidly grow your church? Have you felt squeezed by the people you lead into starting a new program? This may tempt you into trying to entice people to work toward those goals. The goals themselves are not what are bad; it is the way that these goals were conceived in your spirit. The key is in your motives. Are you motivated by the pressure or a desire to fulfill the will of God? Think twice, and pray more, before you answer that question. Pressure makes people do all kinds of things.

On the contrary, keeping a proper perspective on how to use reward power will go a long way in motivating and mobilizing people. Now, rewards in the kingdom of God come in different forms. For example, if you see that your youth pastor has been faithful to the work and has shown strong leadership evidenced in the spiritual and physical growth of the youth group, it may motivate you to give him the opportunity to add youth services in the main sanctuary. Another example would be if you felt compelled to promote a minister in your church to some level of pastorate. Rewarding with wealth would be if you feel prompted to allow other trusted leaders to have and run their own accounts, giving them full access to needed funds.

All of these things could and should be used *only* for the edification of the body of Christ and the glory of God. If it does not fit this mold, then throw it out because we should only be concerned about the direction that God wants us to follow. This includes the programs, handling of funds, organizational structure of the church, among many other things. That is proper practice of reward power. However, if you did these things just to lighten your workload so you can spend more time off or on the golf course, then I suggest you check yourself. Such motives may end up moving you to do some questionable things. What follows are examples of leaders that have used reward power justly and unjustly.

☙

Biblical and Historical Examples

There is a plethora of examples of solely using reward power to motivate followers throughout history. Paul tells us that the all-out pursuit of financial gain causes nothing but sorrow and grief (see 1 Timothy 6:10). So, why would we want to create a reward system that could foster this very thing? The Bible records many of these instances, but one in particular stands out.

The Queen and Her Focus

The Queen of Sheba is an interesting biblical character. Seemingly out of nowhere, she enters the scene in 2 Chronicles 9. The Bible records her entrance this way, "And when the queen of Sheba heard of the fame of Solomon, she came to prove Solomon with hard questions at Jerusalem, with a very great company, and camels that bare spices, and gold in abundance, and precious stones" (2 Chronicles 9:1). Notice, that Solomon's fame or status is what prompted her to travel all that way just to talk to him. She was attracted to his status, not the fact that he was the king of Israel, the storied nation that God brought out from Egypt with a mighty hand.

She didn't note him first for his dedication to his God or the ability to keep peace all around his kingdom. It doesn't appear that she had any initial spiritual interest at all. In fact, everything that she seemed to be impressed with was temporal. It was evident that she valued the acquiring of tangible "rewards." It was riches, earthly gain that caused her to praise the Lord!

I find it interesting that she was so fascinated by king Solomon's servants. She marveled at how happy and joyful they were to serve the king. Could this be because she had not seen this before? Was she used to her servants complaining all the time? Did she use phrases like, "you just can't find good help these days" upon finding out that some had left their posts? It is impossible to tell exactly, but it could have been the case. Could it be that her reward system was faulty?

Dedicated people don't work for the kingdom in order to make a quick buck. Now, don't misunderstand me. The Bible says that the one working the field should be the "first partaker of the fruits" (2 Timothy 2:6) and not to "muzzle the ox that treadeth out the corn, the labourer is worthy of his reward" (1 Timothy 5:18). It is perfectly biblical and mandated by God that full-time ministers get paid if the funds are available. That is not what I am talking about. I am talking about a reward system that is based solely on tangible things.

Thankfully, I don't see a major problem with this in the church . . . that is right now. But I fear that as the days continue and the Lord tarries, a generation of leaders will rise up who will not know how to motivate and mobilize volunteers by casting a powerful vision and teaching them that the reward is in the work. If the reward system becomes based upon the wrong things, then eventually it will contribute more to an "entitlement" culture instead of a grateful and satisfied generation. The latter is what Solomon was able to build. The former appears to be the main way in which the Queen of Sheba chose to reward and honor. The Bible records the queen's greeting of king Solomon as littered with pomp and circumstance and full of monetary and tangible gifts. After she hears Solomon's wisdom and sees the wonders of his kingdom as described earlier, she gives him more money. Now, I know that it was customary for this to happen, but there is no denying that power and financial rewards was what made her tick; it was planted firmly in her heart.

Notice something else. She had to ask that Solomon give her stuff! 2 Chronicles 9:12 states, "And king Solomon gave to the queen of Sheba all her desire, whatsoever she asked, beside that which she had brought unto the king." Some think that Solomon gave her his wisdom in writing, however, based on her focus upon tangible things, I believe it was a monetary gift. Also, the wording here is interesting. It says, "all her desire, whatsoever she asked, beside that which she had brought unto the king." This makes it sound like she asked that Solomon reward her with the very things, or at least similar things, as she had brought him.

Her focus on a monetary reward system appears to have fostered a culture of contempt among her palace. We can only infer these things from Scripture. However, it goes without saying that trying to motivate followers solely by what you can reward them with is like being on a horse that walks only because you have a carrot strung out in front of him! As we will see, Solomon's kingdom was not built this way.

Solomon and His Influence
We dissed Solomon's demise in chapter 3, but there were several things that he did right. One was how

he motivated people to work in the kingdom. It is true that King Solomon built a marvelous kingdom full of wonder and wealth. However, his focus was not on monetary things, at least not in the beginning. His prayer upon taking the throne famously signifies the beginning of his prosperity (see 2 Chronicles 1:7-10). However, the willingness of the kingdom to follow his lead started way before that.

Solomon was made king before David passed away. David was one of the most beloved kings in the history of Israel. You would think there would be sorrow when he left office. You would think that there would be at least some objections from the people. There was a dispute in the family, but as far as we can tell from the language of the Bible, we see joy and gladness when Solomon assumed the throne (see 1 Chronicles 29:21-25).

How could this be? It was because he knew how to build powerful relationships with people. Everyone appeared to like him. His influencing power at that time did not rest in how he could reward the people. They served him and the kingdom because of who he was and what he meant to them! He was the beloved ambassador of Israel. Isn't that how you want people to serve the kingdom? It begins by not asking yourself what you can give someone in order to foster motivation. It begins with building trust and relationships with the people you lead. He paid those that he had to appoint to official positions, but it appears that he kept everything in perspective. He knew how to ask for help. He knew how to cast vision. He knew how to motivate. No one murmured about recognition or wanting a promotion like they did with Moses (see Numbers 16). No one arbitrarily left their post like Demas did with Paul (see 2 Timothy 4:10).

Does this make the leadership of Paul and Moses ineffective? Not at all, but the children of Israel didn't exactly walk around in the wilderness with joy and great gladness like they did serving Solomon, did they? You might say, "different people, different times." Yeah, I get it. However, as a leader in the kingdom of God, you will encounter all sorts of people. It is your task to remain faithful to God so you can take all of these personalities, nationalities, backgrounds, and specialties and make them function as a well-oiled vehicle that is just happy to be on the road!

What is more valuable love and support or tangible rewards? If you only motivate people with tangible rewards, some will follow, but they may not be those whom you want. However, through integrity and love, if you support, develop, and prosper those you lead and cast a powerful shared vision, they will die for you. Obviously, this is the difference between the very foundations of the two different reward systems that a leader can build. Is it solely built on things, or is it based on the powerful fact that the reward truly is in the work? We have to make sure that we steer the people's heart in the right direction. This direction is not the wealth-focused priority of the South. It comes from the Lord. People go to the place from which you call them. A leader doesn't point and say, "go." A leader goes and then says, "come, I know the way."

☙❧

Closing and Transition

There are many more examples of this throughout history—especially in the Bible. They all have one common denominator. Those who were truly successful, who gained true and genuine followers, not just people along for the ride, built a foundation that was sure. It was founded upon a rock. That rock is the true love of God that moves the leader to genuinely seek the spiritual, emotional, and mental prosperity of those he leads. This is leading with empowerment from God and the direction from which you call others.

Chapter Six

A Common Theme: Referent Power and Flawed Diplomacy

"Leadership to me means duty, honor, country. It means character, and it means listening from time to time"
— GEORGE W. BUSH

W hen looking over the vast sea of history that spreads through the ages, we can see that virtually every nation has at least one thing in common. All nations, from the beginning of civilization to now, employ the power of diplomacy. They do this for many reasons.

Perhaps they want to form a trade deal. Or maybe they wish to mitigate a skirmish between nations. Whatever the goal, diplomacy has proved to be a powerful tool among global interactions.

Diplomacy has been successfully used in this world to solve all kinds of problems. There is something to be said about the power of effective communication. If the pen is mightier than the sword, then effective communication is like the skilled swordsman that wields it. Diplomacy is a needed skill as a leader in the church as well. You will be called on from time to time to put out some fires, bring people to consensus, and even negotiate (especially if you are a pastor of a church that has a board!).

In terms of diplomacy, a leader can find his source from any of the directions prior to this chapter. You can communicate from the East and find the basis of your communication resting on expert power, thinking you are the smartest person in the room. You can speak in a condescending tone and try to coerce people and groups into submission, communicating from the West. Or, you can even communicate from the South, attempting to reward someone with some kind of bribe or exchange for a favor.

As noted in all prior chapters, we have the God-given power to exercise each form of power if we keep it in the right context. We can't focus on any one of these forms of power, because to trust solely on them is to not trust solely on God but in the flesh. Isn't this the foundational reason why Moses was unable to enter the Promised Land (see Numbers 20:8-13)? Just for a split second, he stopped trusting in the Word of God and trusted on his own merit. It cost him dearly. We need to learn the art of effective communication, but this too can become a crutch, if we trust in it alone.

ℰℵ

Referent Power Defined

Referent power is typically defined as a leader's ability to attract and motivate followers based on who he knows. It involves relationships. Oftentimes, people who already have a lot of friends don't have trouble making new friends because they are popular and people want to know them. This trait can be used for good or bad. For example, a new kid to a school may want so badly to be part of a popular group that they will do anything to befriend one of those in the group. In such a scenario the popular kid has a great deal of referent power. However, this doesn't always work out too well. Why, you ask? Well, sometimes the popular kid is a jerk and only invites the new kid to be part of the clique because they are going to play some prank on him. Now, you can call me cynical if you want, but it happens. In this simple example, the popular kid used his referent power to get the new kid to do something he wanted him to do. However, the end result is embarrassment for the new kid and detention (or possibly worse) for the popular kid.

Maybe this example isn't exactly one we might find every day in the church. But it is sufficient enough to describe referent power. It all hinges on your motives and intentions. Do you only want to get some personal gain out of a relationship, or do you seek to bring God glory while allowing yourself to decrease and Him to increase? Let me give you another example. How about a youth pastor who desperately needs another person to come to a fund-raising event on Saturday. He looks over and sees a young man that he knows has been praying about being called into the ministry. He has even discussed it with his pastor. This youth pastor may be tempted to ask that young man to cancel his plans for that day, come to the fund-raising event, and in return he will give a glowing review of his character and "endorse" him, so to speak, to the senior pastor. See how that works? The young man wants to obey the youth pastor because he is his department leader. However, he may be tempted to oblige just because of who the youth pastor is close to. Now, we absolutely should give credit where credit is due; that is biblical. However, we need to be mindful of our motives at all times. Did the youth pastor elevate the young man because he saw God in him, or did he do it because the young man complied to his wishes? Furthermore, did the young man agree to come to the fundraising event only for the benefit that he would get in return?

If we are not careful as leaders, we can find ourselves trying to motivate for the wrong reasons. That young man should get a good report from his youth pastor based solely on his faithfulness, character, and walk with God not the fact that he did his leader a favor. Now, I know that being faithful often means cancelling your plans for the house of God, however, I cannot stress enough that this whole principle is based on the leader's (and the followers to some extent) motives and intentions. It's about what we have in our heart, and how it manifests itself on the outside.

∽

Referent Power from the East

Today, Christian leaders (and I use this term loosely) are often looked at as intellectuals to a degree. They are viewed as having a great deal of wisdom and knowledge. In this day and age, it is not uncommon for pastors and ministers to have doctorate degrees, write books, and be recognized as leaders in their community. This is all great if it generally bolsters the kingdom of God. I applaud anyone that will spend a great deal of their years dedicated to the study of something that they intend to use to propagate the gospel. However, motives play a huge role here, too.

During the course of their career, a minister's intellect and wisdom may afford him the opportunity to build a vast network with powerful people. What are the intentions of building this network? Do you want to fellowship with the body of Christ? Do you want to be able to point people that you meet in other cities to churches where you know they will get saved and spiritually fed? Or do you want to grow your network because you want to spread the word on how smart you are? Do you want to create a platform for yourself? That's not leadership; that's self-aggrandizement. Isn't this how Absalom made his insurrection?

King David's son Absalom was very subtle. We see this in how he devised a plan to kill his brother Amnon as well as when he knew just what to do to get Joab's attention after he had unsuccessfully called for him twice (see 2 Samuel 13 and 14).

In 2 Samuel 15 we see how Absalom devised a plan to take the throne. He sat in the gate, where business was usually conducted. There, he would notice those having disputes who needed arbitration. His thought process was to use his intellect to be their judge. Since they knew he was the king's son, he had a great deal of referent power. They trusted him because of who he knew, and who he knew made him great to them.

It was here that he "stole the hearts of the men of Israel" (2 Samuel 15:6). During this time, he met more influential people. Those influential people gave him more referent power while he exercised his expert power. See how intellect and referent power can work in conjunction to bring division in the kingdom? His motives were anything but pure. His insurrection caused much grief, heartache, death, and destruction. All of this just because he wanted to build his network to show everyone why he should be in charge.

As leaders in the kingdom of God, we shouldn't stoop so low. If you have to spiritually stoop down, then spiritually you are much farther from the top than when you started. Leading this way reeks of arrogance. But Proverbs 18:12 tells us that arrogance is the precursor to failure. The same chapter gives the best advice in terms of using your intellect to build relationships for personal gain: "A man's gift maketh room for him, and bringeth him before great men. He that is first in his own cause seemeth just; but his neighbour cometh and searcheth him" (Proverbs 18:16-17).

The word *searcheth* in verse 17 means "to be found out." If you stay in the will of God and keep everything in the proper perspective by only seeking to give Him glory and further His kingdom, then God will make you stand out among your peers. He wants model leadership to be displayed. However, don't think that you are fooling anyone by the false humility you use to heap praise and power upon yourself. The connections we make are supposed to strengthen the kingdom of God not tear it apart. Additionally, relationships shouldn't be for the sole purpose of building up your address book so you can tell everyone what a big shot you are. First, seek righteousness in the kingdom, and everything else will fall into place (see Matthew 6:33).

ﾟ

Referent Power from the West

Historically, Western nations, especially ancient Greece and Rome, have placed much stock in government, diplomacy, and politicking. Such was the case in the days prior to Julius Caesar becoming emperor and continued in some form during and after his reign. The Roman government had become a playground for political maneuvering. What started as the foundation of democracy ended up being an entirely different system founded upon under-handed deals and claims of "life will be better with me in charge because I know all the right people."

This bred a form of leadership in Rome that closely resembled how the nation conquered their

foes, with an iron fist. However, Dwight D. Eisen-
hower once said, "You don't lead by hitting people
over the head — that's assault, not leadership."
In the church, we don't find pastors and other
leaders physically beating their followers. No, in
the church we see this as more of a manipulation
of emotions, desires, and ideals. In other words, it's
spiritually based.

During their expansion before, during, and
after Christ, the Romans were able to subdue many
nations simply through diplomacy. A diplomat
would travel to a far land and meet with the powers
of that nation. They basically would have just one
offer: willingly come under the authority of Roman
rule, become a vassal, or be forcefully taken over and
suffer much destruction and death. In the church,
we can find ourselves leading in a similar fashion.

It may sound cynical, but there are those even
in the kingdom of God who think the best way to
go about getting what you want is to try to manipulate people. Most of the time, I believe that they
don't even realize what they're doing. It's probably
a function of how they were taught (or what they
caught) from prior leadership. In any case, we
need to become consciously aware of the fact that

leadership involves the stewardship of souls. With that comes the stewardship of fragile emotions, desires, and dreams of the people under our care. If we are not careful, we can use people as a tool to manipulate rather than develop. In this way, souls become nothing more than a means to an end. In terms of referent power, a leader can manipulate with the power of his connections. Oftentimes, someone might seek out a relationship with another person because they want to exert their power. They seek to pass themselves off as a royal monarch rather than a royal priesthood (servanthood). However, this adds nothing to the kingdom of God. How do you think God feels about this attitude? One need not look any further than when Jesus rebuked James and John for wanting to call fire down from heaven on people that did not welcome him (see Luke 9:51-56)

This came right after one of the disciple's disputes about who should be the greatest (see Luke 9:46-48). Obviously, Jesus' explanation of kingdom hierarchy in verse 48 did not sink in or else they would have showed a little more humility. This time, Jesus turned around and sharply rebuked them for their desire to use their coercive power just to make an example of somebody. He poignantly said, "Ye know not what manner of spirit ye are of. For the Son of man is not come to destroy men's lives, but to save them" (Luke 9:55-56). He rebuked them for what they had in their heart.

What's even more indicting, though, is that they didn't even know what they were actually saying and doing! Leading from your "high horse" will do nothing except force compliance and create a culture of contempt. No one is royalty in the kingdom of God. In fact, the Bible tells us that there is only one Potentate, namely Jesus our King of kings and Lord of lords (see 1 Timothy 6:15). Again, this all can be avoided by having the right motives and intentions while keeping a genuinely humble spirit.

Ask yourself, "Why do I want to get close to people in authority?" Is it because you hold them to be a figure from which to learn more about God? Is it because you want more fellowship with the ministers of God? Or, do you wish to make these relationships because you want to get to the top of the ministry ladder as fast as you can? Ministry and leadership are not to be boiled down to the prestige of your professional network, or with whom you can rub shoulders. Pray that God will always allow you to have a genuinely humble spirit and pure motives, so you don't end up exposed like the sons of Sceva who knew all the right people but had no real power at all (see Acts 19:13-16).

∽

Referent Power from the South

Recall that leading solely with reward power is like placing a priority on how you can reward and entice people much like the ancient kingdoms that lie south of Jerusalem. Referent power can work in conjunction with reward power when we try to use our network or contacts and relationships to persuade others. How can this happen, you say? Have you ever been involved in a ministerial election at a conference? There is much political maneuvering involved.

It is natural, at least to a certain extent, to get excited and feel honored that you know and have a relationship with influential people. However, we cross the line when we seek these relationships because we want to use them to entice people to follow our leadership. You will find people that will want to get close to you because you know some powerful people. First of all, they shouldn't seek your friendship if it's all about using you as a stepping stone. However, we can't control the actions of other's, nor do we really know what is in their heart at any given time. We only have control over what we do and for what reason we do it.

A good example of this principle of seeking influence and power is found in the book of Esther. Haman desperately wanted to be a powerful man, so he made all the right relationships. Eventually, he climbed his way to the top of the royal class (see Esther 3). This gave him an even bigger platform and put him in the company of many other influential people. He became so great in the Persian kingdom that others bowed to him. It is important to note that they did not do this of their own accord. No, they bowed because they were commanded to do so (see Esther 3:2).

Now Haman constantly had his eyes on Mordecai. He resented the fact that God seemed to bless Mordecai even though he would not bow down to him. When you lead by trying to promote yourself and show people that you are "worth" following, you will constantly find yourself trying to "keep up with the Joneses" positionally. You will always have your eyes on someone else, or the next step up, and how you can get there.

When you seek promotion based on growing your network and becoming as powerful as you can, it only breeds coercion as I described in chapter 4 of this book. Leading like this will only leave you frustrated. Nothing good, spiritual or otherwise, can come from coercion. Because of lack of compliance, Haman was moved with such indignation that he thought to destroy God's people! Always remember that God's people will be affected in the crossfire between you and your pursuit for prestige.

The end of Haman was anything but glorious. He wound up getting hanged on the same instrument from which he wished to assert his power—the gallows that he prepared for Mordecai! The biggest takeaway here is that leading this way will ultimately destroy you. You may get to where you want, but in the process, you will forfeit your integrity.

On the contrary, Mordecai did things right. He sought the prosperity of the kingdom of God not his own. God used this to put him in the very position that Haman sought. As a matter of fact, Mordecai wound up in a higher place of leadership than Haman (see Ester 9). Since Mordecai led from the right direction and spirit, genuine commitment was automatically the result. As said earlier, seek the kingdom of God first in all you do, and God will put you where you need to be when you need to be there.

☙

Closing and Transition

Referent power can be used in conjunction with any of the other forms of power. You can use your relationships to subtly lure, outright coerce and manipulate, and persuade people to follow your leadership. However, is that really what you want? This is pseudo-leadership. When people follow you for any reason other than your anointing and walk with God, the best you can hope for is mere compliance. You will never transcend that boundary to enlist their full commitment.

Furthermore, blatantly seeking relationships with influential people for any disingenuous intention will only leave you exposed and lonely (see Proverbs 18:16-17; Acts 19:13-16). God should be the center of all things, and His will not our own prosperity should be our chief motivation. Whether you are motivated by climbing the ministerial ladder or to just enjoy swaying people toward your own ambitions, it merits nothing if you don't see first to bring God glory. You can't serve God and yourself at the same time (see Matthew 6:24).

People will be drawn to you because of who you represent, much like the diplomats in the previous section. But, do you want people to follow your lead because you represent intelligence, supremacy, or some personal benefit, or do you want people to genuinely follow you based on your anointing and walk with God? The later yields powerful teams like those Nehemiah rallied (see Nehemiah 4:6). They truly bought in to the vision of the leadership because Nehemiah had pure and genuine intentions. This goes for the relationships within a particular church as well as a network of minister's like one would find in a religious organization.

Chapter Seven

Promotion from the North: Legitimate Power and Authentic Leadership

"For promotion cometh neither from the east, nor from the west, nor from the south. But God is the judge: he putteth down one, and setteth up another"
— PSALM 75:6-7

And so, we come to the crux of the matter. What does spiritually empowered leadership really look like? Well, if you have paid attention, it has been woven through the fabric of this book from the very beginning. Every form of power can be used the wrong way or the right way.

The key is in understanding where the reference point is in relation to the East (expert power), West (coercive power), and South (reward power).

༈

Significance of the North

You may wonder why Asaph (or, most likely, David) left out the North in his description of where promotion comes from. In his commentary on the Bible, Matthew Henry suggests that in those days the North was reserved for that secret place from which God's wisdom and counsel comes. The funny thing about the North is that all other directions are relative to it. When the mariners of old navigated the vast seas of the world, they used Polaris as a reference point. Polaris is better known as the North Star. The Holy Ghost acts like the North Star for leaders seeking direction. After all, Peter refers to Jesus as the day star. The term *day star* comes from the Greek word *phosphoros* meaning, "light bringing" or "light giving." It refers to how Jesus shines light in our lives and gives us revelation.

Leading from the North involves us getting in tune with the Spirit and navigating to the place from which God is calling. Once we receive that vision and plan from God, it's our job to help others navigate to the same place. This process should continue over and over, so everyone is constantly moving in the same direction: toward God. Of course, navigation usually requires us to understand and even use the other directions at our disposal.

We may have to refer to the East in order to shed light on some issue or give a much deeper understanding of the Word to someone else. Additionally, we may have to look toward the West to rebuke sin and exercise spiritual authority. We may also have to look to the South to make sure that we are giving credit where it is due. However, referencing these directions, or forms of power if you will, while moving toward the North is a completely different thing than actually leading from them. If God is calling from the North, then leading from any other way is contrary. Honing in on these directions will get us lost in the journey to lead people closer to God. It will only lead God's people astray.

Before doing anything, it is a good idea to pray and reflect (see 2 Corinthians 13:5). If you are genuinely (and be honest now) headed toward and focusing on God, then you are using a form of leadership power known as legitimate power, and all other forms of power will fit nicely into place. You will know when and how to use each of them appropriately because it will be divinely inspired.

⚬⚭⚬

Legitimate Power Defined

Legitimate power in the business realm simply means that a leader has been recognized by the organization to lead in the capacity in which he or she is stationed. However, legitimate power looks different in the church. While it is important for us to be recognized by bishops, elders, and pastors as leaders, a title or position is not the be-all and end-all.Legitimate power in the church starts long before one is given a title, if ever. See, you don't have to have a title in the church to possess legitimate power. The main criterion is this: you must be recognized by God.

When people have a divine call to leadership, it manifests itself in anointing and spiritual gifts. Specific gifts could include administration, leadership, and organization, just to name a few, that may accompany a genuinely called and chosen leader (see 1 Corinthians 12:28; Romans 12:8). It is important to know that God will make these gifts stand out, and you will find favor with the leaders that have been placed over you (see Proverbs 18:16). But the overwhelming prerequisite is that you must be filled and overflowing with the Holy Ghost. Let's take a look at what actually happened to Jesus' followers when they were filled with the Holy Ghost.

Recall that Jesus told them to go and remain in Jerusalem until they were "endued with power" (Luke 24:49). The word *endued* means "to invest in by clothing someone." When God promotes us into leadership, He clothes us with the necessary power to fulfill our office. We don't have to do anything to promote ourselves or use self-aggrandizing means to make sure people notice who we are. God's true power is recognized in individuals that He anoints and separates for His purpose.

Think about it. Peter, before he was "endued with power" was a bold person. However, his boldness didn't really get him anywhere except for the revelation of Christ that he proclaimed in Matthew 16:16. He had a certain amount of power or influence before he got the Holy Ghost, as did the rest of disciples (see Matthew 10). However, he rarely used this empowerment for good. One time we find him cutting someone's ear off (see Matthew 26:51). In another place we see him cursing up a storm and emphatically denying that he even knew Jesus (see Matthew 26:69-75). Finally, once Jesus died, he was so overwhelmed that the only thing he could think to do is go back to his former occupation (see John 21:3).

This proves that we can know God, have a revelation of who He is, and at the same time not really understand how to use the power that He gives us. Jesus told them back in Matthew 10 that he gave them power. But I don't see where they really used it the way it was intended. I believe that was by design, though.

Notice what Jesus said after he told them that he gave them this power. He began to speak about what would happen to them after he ascended into heaven. He told them that they would be delivered to councils, whipped, and brought before governments (see Matthew 10:17-18). All of these things actually did happen to them but only after Jesus ascended and the Holy Ghost fell on them in Acts 2. In essence, Jesus knew that they wouldn't receive true power until they were "endued with power from on high" (Luke 24:49).

See, when we lead strictly from our own merit, we fail as leaders. And we potentially rob His people of the vision that God has for their lives collectively and individually. Even leading from the gifts that God has given us through the Holy Ghost will not work if we solely trust in them. It then becomes a foundation built upon the gifts and not the gift Giver. It's a foundation of shifting sand that will not hold once we begin to build on top of it. Building upon the Rock that is Christ should be our top priority even in the construction of our own leadership house (see Matthew 7:24-27).

We absolutely need to use the gifts and talents that we inherently possess in conjunction with those gifts God gives us through the Holy Ghost. However, we need to understand that we can't trust in our intellect, gift of gab, or any spiritual gift as sufficient enough by themselves to foster genuine spiritual leadership. We have to wholeheartedly depend on the Holy Ghost to empower us. Only then can we see clearly enough to apply all the other principles. Proverbs 22:4 says, "By humility and the fear of the LORD are riches, and honour, and life."

Therefore, being filled with the Holy Ghost, allowing God to work through you is the true definition of being "endued with power" or empowered. And as we will see, it is possible to use the other forms of leadership power appropriately through the lens of the Spirit and not the flesh.

∞

Legitimate Expert Power

Upon being filled with the Holy Ghost, Peter and the rest of the disciples were never the same. Suddenly, they were empowered to take on the world but not through their own power. They were supernaturally empowered by God to lead the masses to Him. One of the ways God did this was to give them supernatural expert power. Acts 4 tells a compelling story in this regard. Many people can readily remember the story in the previous chapter about how the lame man was healed at the Beautiful Gate. However, chapter 4 reveals the trial that the apostles had to go through as a result of working in their God-given leadership post.

Upon preaching the name of Jesus, they were immediately seized and put in prison. When their captors began to question them, Peter boldly lifted up his voice (in similar fashion as he had done in times past without the Holy Ghost). However, this time, Luke makes a point to tell us that what proceeded out of his mouth was ordained and given to him by the Spirit. Not only did Peter begin to preach to them in the Name of Jesus, but he also quoted a rather hidden prophecy concerning the Messiah. Peter told them that Jesus is "the stone which was set at nought of you builders, which is become the head of the corner" (Acts 4:11). This prophecy is originally found in Psalms 118:22. Jesus also quoted this prophecy in the presence of his disciples in Matthew 21:42; an account that is also told in the Gospel of Mark and the Gospel of Luke.

This one account among many shows the power, as well as the empowerment, of the Holy Ghost. Peter was never seen quoting this much Scripture and using his boldness to preach and open spiritual doors before he was filled and ordained by God. Messianic prophecies found in the Psalms can be somewhat obscure and hidden. However, the Spirit readily called this to Peter's mind when needed. Jesus told his disciples that once he came back as the manifested Holy Ghost and filled them, that he would bring all the things that he had taught them to their memory (see John 14:26). This is the life transforming power of the Holy Ghost in action.

Luke recorded something very interesting upon Peter's closing. He says that the educated priestly class "perceived that they were unlearned and ignorant men" (Acts 4:13). This does not mean that the apostles showed themselves to be fools before the Sanhedrin. On the contrary, the religious rulers took notice of the apostles' posture and confidence, their boldness as they quoted Scripture that showed Jesus to be the Christ. They looked at these men who had no formal training in the law and Scripture, and they marveled at how much they knew.

However, the apostles didn't just rattle off a bunch of Scripture just to look smart. No, they had a purpose. That purpose was to first glorify God by proclaiming that Jesus is the Messiah. This priority took center stage even in the midst of extreme pressure and trial. Their expert power was governed and bridled by the Holy Ghost and used appropriately. This glorified God from beginning to end. There were no ill motives, side benefits, or selfish gain. And, the kingdom of God flourished as a result.

One of the most interesting pointsabout this story is the apostles did not have to boast about their knowledge to get the point across. Peter spoke what was given to him by the Spirit, nothing more, nothing less. He did not have to give a dissertation. In fact, he preached more and gave more Scripture to the masses that he helped convert in Acts 2 and 3. He did it that way then because the Holy Ghost told him to do so, and it was no different this time.

However, such a small discourse yielded exactly what God wanted. Acts 4:13 goes on to say, "they took knowledge of them, that they had been with Jesus." This is powerful! How many people were going around just supposing Jesus to be the Christ and giving scriptural evidence? I tend to think there were countless people proclaiming Jesus as the Messiah. There had to be. At that point in time the Bible recorded 8,120 people that had been saved. But what was different about Peter?

They didn't recognize him as having been with Jesus at first. It wasn't until they recognized his anointing and the fact that he did not receive his understanding of Scripture from formal training as they had. His expert power was governed by the legitimate power of the Holy Ghost that was imparted to him to fulfill God's purpose in God's time, not his own.

 exo

Legitimate Coercive Power

Just like expert power, there is a point in time where the anointing of God's servants and coercive power intersect. One may be inclined to think that a humble servant of God should never use coercive power. However, this is simply not the case. God does not want pushovers as leaders in His kingdom. Pushovers become puppets that are easily manipulated and persuaded by other people who are motivated by selfish intentions.

Coercive power can almost be a misleading term because the word *coercive* sounds like it implies some kind of manipulation. However, that is not exactly the definition of coercive power for spiritual leaders. When used appropriately, coercive power is just a term used to describe a leader's ability to persuade those they lead. This can be done through manipulation, and sadly it happens often. However, when its bridled by the Holy Ghost, coercive power is actually just simply exercising the spiritual authority that God has imparted. But it must be done biblically.

Look at Paul for instance. He consistently expressed his love for the churches. However, there were certain times when he had to exercise his spiritual authority in order to deal with some issue. The Corinthian church is notorious for being one of the most carnal. Paul starts his first letter to them by wishing them grace (see 1 Corinthians 1:3). However, he eventually lays in to them for their acceptance of sin (see 1 Corinthians 5). It is important to note that Paul set a major precedent in terms of coercive power and its use in spiritual leadership.

The key point is found in 1 Corinthians 4:14-16, which states,

> I write not these things to shame you, but as my beloved sons I warn you. For though ye have ten thousand instructers in Christ, yet have ye not many fathers: for in Christ Jesus I have begotten you through the gospel. Wherefore I beseech you, be ye followers of me.

Before Paul upbraids them for their carnality, he lets them know his motives and intentions. He did not call them out and embarrass them in front of people just to make an example out of them. Nor, did he feel the need to puff himself up and intimidate them, so he could remain on some kind of spiritual high horse. No, he simply did it out of his godly love for them. The expression of love is not the absence of punishment or rebuke. This is where many people go wrong in many relationships, including those in the church, within the family, and beyond.

The fact is that expressions of love sometimes include those actions that may seem harsh on the surface, but they work toward that person's overall good. An example would be how God allows certain things in our lives in order to build character and bring us closer to Him (see 2 Corinthians 4:16-17; Hebrews 12:5-11). However, none of us would dare use this as evidence to accuse God of hating us, would we? Now, if we don't foolishly charge God for disciplining us, then why would we not think that sometimes leaders have to do the same thing to their congregants?

See, Paul's motives rested on getting the Corinthian church to heaven and making sure that God was not blasphemed because of their actions. This is the proper motive behind using coercive power. Many leaders seek to twist people's arms in order to get something done or get them to do something they want. This is not proper coercive power. I don't see anywhere where Paul threatened or tried to intimidate to get his point across. He kept everything in perspective and centered in the love of God. Paul was truly standing on his God-given authority. At the same time, his genuine love for his followers propelled him to act as their spiritual father.

If we are going to use the spiritual authority that God has given, it must be inspired and governed by the Holy Ghost. The fact that God has given us power and authority to shepherd His flock is not an excuse to mistreat the souls that God has given us to lead. Empowerment means that God has entrusted us. Can He count on us to bridle our authority and use it appropriately when dealing with people? There will be times when we have no choice but to assert our spiritual authority, for we don't bear the sword in vain (see Romans 13:4). But love should be the overarching and prevailing theme even in those times.

✃

Legitimate Reward Power

Reward power is hard to define within the church. This is because when someone mentions rewards, most people automatically think about money or something of tangible benefit to them. However, we rely so much on volunteer work in the church, that we often overlook the fact that all leaders, including spiritual leaders, have been given reward power as a tool to influence people. Like all other forms of power, we can misuse reward power in many ways including, but not limited to, those examples described in chapter 5. As leaders, we must recognize this empowerment and use it for the glory of God and the propagation of His kingdom.

Sadly, so many people are starving for recognition and/or to get put on paid staff. They have forgotten that the best reward is having done the work of the Lord itself. The reward is in the work. As leaders, we must successfully ingrain this thinking in those we lead. If not, we will create a group of people who will want some sort of reward for everything they do for the kingdom. Now, I do understand that the Word tells us to render "tribute to whom tribute is due" (Romans 13:7). However, if we are not careful, we can create a culture of receiving instead of a culture of giving.

While we must understand that we have the power to motivate others by using our God-given reward power, it is important that we not put a great deal of emphasis in handing out rewards in whatever form: recognition, promotion, financial. Many take this principle too far in that they never give praise, recognition, and honor to those who do a job well done or put people that they know are called and faithful on paid staff (that is if the church needs it and can afford it).

While the Bible instructs us to be wise and not to create a culture that focuses attention away from God, Proverbs 3:27 also says to, "withhold not good from them to whom it is due, when it is in the power of thine hand to do it." The second part of this verse is key. The power, that is reward power, and its proper use is the leader's responsibility. It is in our power to reward or not reward, but the Bible tells us not to withhold it from people that deserve it.

People need to know that they are valued. This does more than tickle the ego. Letting people know that they are valued gives a sense of security in the kingdom. It helps people know that they are going in the right direction. Remember, it is the leader's responsibility to make sure everyone is on course to make it to the place where God is calling us.

When James, Peter, and John perceived or discerned that God had called Paul, they gave him him "the right hands of fellowship" (Galatians 2:9). In this act there are found several points about the proper use of reward power.

First, we must understand that this was an act of recognition. The apostles openly recognized Paul and Barnabas for their contribution to the kingdom. What does this phrase actually mean? Well, as Apostolic Pentecostals we should know what the "right hand" means. It means a position of authority and honor. The word *fellowship* here means participation or community. Paul and Barnabas were accepted and recognized as leaders in the kingdom of God. The apostles left nothing unsaid. Paul didn't have to guess whether or not he was on the right track.

The apostles used reward power as a means to empower Paul and Barnabas to continue with apostolic authority. This is the biblical way to use reward power to motivate and inspire those you lead. They openly recognized them, accepting them into the ministry. It was a well-deserved reward. Paul, Barnabas, and the apostles kept everything in the right perspective. None sought personal glory. Furthermore, the apostles didn't think about trying to manipulate and withhold the good reward from them.

Now, what were the results? What transpired from this was empowered, confident, and anointed leadership that reached the entire known world with the gospel. Countless millions are still receiving the gospel as a result of this one display of appreciation and acceptance. The leaders had it in their power to recognize and reward, and they did. They didn't ignore it, nor did they make some big show in order to put someone on a pedestal of glory. There is balance in this as well as a purpose that will give honor to where it is due and at the same time ultimately give God all the glory.

༄

Legitimate Referent Power

Recall that referent power refers to the leader's ability to build personal relationships. As discussed in chapter 6, referent power can be used for personal gain or to build the kingdom of God. The important thing is to always do everything with pure motives and the ultimate intent to bring God glory. God didn't tell us that whatsoever we do, do it in the name of yourself. He told us that "whatsoever ye do, do all in the name of the Lord Jesus" (Colossians 3:17).

Using referent power can have us leading from any one of the four directions, but only one is genuine and powerful enough to sustain true apostolic leadership. Easterly, westerly, and southerly leadership will not be sufficient to propel and sustain a successful ministry that fosters physical, spiritual, and emotional growth. Only a focus on God and His plans will suffice. This is the beginning of genuine spiritual leadership, and it is characterized by humility and submission to Him. If we can't submit to Him, then people will have a hard time trusting us enough to submit to our leadership. This is what makes leading from the North so powerful.

Leading from the East with referent power will move you to think you can build relationships solely on your intellect. It will create arrogance not the type of humility that is required of God's servants. Proverbs 22:4 tells us that, "by humility and the fear of the LORD are riches, and honour, and life." When you push your intellect to the forefront, you supplant the countenance and anointing that God has placed on you. This is because it is an act that shows God you are not dependent upon Him.

Anything less than being fully dependent on God is unbelief and an outward declaration of lack of faith in the operation of God in our lives. In other words, we are saying we don't need the direction of the Holy Ghost. As a result we place ourselves in a standoffish position with God and, therefore, are not teachable and not pliable. So when we push our intellect forward for all to see in a disingenuous and arrogant way, we are actually saying, "it's okay God, I got this!" God is more than willing to let you have the reins for a while so you can see just how much you need Him. However, those that fall prey to this deception generally begin to think that everyone else is to blame when faced with challenges in their ministry.

This just simply will not work in God's economy. His idea of leadership is markedly different than this easterly leadership. Matthew 23:12 says, "whosoever shall exalt himself shall be abased; and he that shall humble himself shall be exalted." This is significant because Jesus rebukes the Pharisees immediately after he makes this statement. The Pharisees were the spiritual leaders of the day, but he rebuked their arrogance.

Jesus called attention to the fact that they were so busy placing themselves on pedestals that they neglected their true spiritual responsibility. As those responsible for leading people to God, they failed miserably because they refused to even make an unbiased investigation into the validity of Jesus ministry and identity. They were too busy aggrandizing their own intelligence in the law, that they became blind to what was right before their eyes. God harshly rebuked them for this. If we are not humble enough to put our own biases aside in submission to His will and plan (or what could be His will and plan), then we will likewise fall and fail.

Similar in principle to the East, you can lead from the West with referent power and think the best way to build relationships is to coerce and manipulate people, beating them into submission so to speak. These leaders come from the school of thought, whether consciously or unconsciously, that leadership is synonymous with dictatorship. However, the people caught in the middle of the struggle for power usually end up hating the dictator and follow out of fear for their life rather than genuine respect and commitment to the leader and the overall cause. No dictator in the history of humanity has ever been able to foster true followership from those they lead.

They truly don't express love for the people, and because of this, they fail to form meaningful relationships that build trust and foster true commitment — the type that will move someone to gladly die (if they must) fighting by your side for the cause that you have instilled in them. Mussolini was killed by his own countrymen; Julius Caesar's Senate conspired against him; and Rehoboam was so abhorred that he caused a civil war.

The Bible explains what is happening in the hearts of dictators who dominate and destroy the people they lead: "And he did evil, because he prepared not his heart to seek the LORD" (2 Chronicles 12:14). This verse is explaining the source of Rehoboam's fall, but it can absolutely describe the foundation of everyone's spiritual demise. People do evil because they don't prepare their heart to seek the Lord.

This is as true in the church as it is out of church. It is obvious that world leaders fall into this category. Just look at the political landscape today. But we fail to recognize it in the church sometimes. No one, even God's called, is exempt from this principle. We must prepare our hearts to seek the Lord. Only then will we have enough love, wisdom, and apostolic (not our own) authority to successfully lead people to the North where God is calling, "Come." We do this by maintaining the proper perspective. We lead with a focus on God, not ourselves. The proper focus coupled with a strong regimen of prayer, fasting, and Bible study will create a powerful link between your heart and God that will be recognized, respected, and ratified by the people you lead.

Finally, we can use our referent power in conjunction with our reward power and fool ourselves into thinking that we can bribe people into a spiritually effective relationship. This can come in many different forms or fashions. It is usually more subtle in the church because we generally don't hear about money exchanged under the table so to speak. However, it can and does happen in many other ways.

Some leaders, for whatever reason, get so insecure about their God-given position that they feel they have to cater to everyone's every need. Others use their status as a means to steer people in the direction they want them to go. Still, other leaders make promises they can't keep hoping to bribe someone into doing their bidding. This may sound harsh, but you would be surprised how easy it is to succumb to a bribe by a pastor. As spiritual leaders with God-given and recognized authority, we get so focused on the task at hand or the end game when moving forward to fulfill the vision that God has instilled in us. Because we are so caught up in the *what*, we often miss the *how*. Why is this important? Well, because what good is it to win the game if you cheated to get there? What good is it that a man could gain the whole world but lose his soul (Mark 8:36-37)?

Leaders with actual power, especially spiritual leaders, can get so close to selling their own soul just because of the "deals" they make. People trust spiritual leaders because they believe that God has put them there to lead them. This is true for legitimate spiritual leadership. However, the leader has a responsibility to nurture, love, and develop that soul not use it as a pawn in some chess match for glory. Success is not defined in the church the same way as in the business world. Success in the business world is founded on profit, which teaches that as long as the business is making money, then anything short of breaking the law (although many cross that line as well) is fair game. Every decision is just a means to an end.

It seems harsh, but if we are not careful, we too can let things like building relationships with the people we lead become just a means to an end. This is also true when it comes to building relationships with colleagues, contemporaries, and those of higher status. Genuine and legitimate spiritual leadership does not stoop so low. Relationships should be built for genuine fellowship and to bring God glory not for personal gain. People are not some pawn or tool you can just use. People are not spiritually disposable or expendable. In the church, success is not defined by the measure of the end game only, but it also is defined by every decision along the way. Integrity is built or destroyed on this very battleground. Every soul is precious, and it matters how we use and what we do with them.

જ્જ

Closing

The sum of the matter is this: leading with legitimate power is to back up and reflect on how and what you are doing with the people that God has placed in your care. Genuine spiritual leadership is not about you, your degree, or your pedigree. It's about your willingness to serve. It's about the people and how you inspire them to get closer to God and His will.

Genuine spiritual leadership is really just anointed servant leadership directed and governed by the Holy Ghost. Servant leadership is so powerful because it actually takes into account the dreams, thoughts, feelings, ambitions, and well-being of those you lead. In fact, spiritual servant leadership is all about these. It is founded completely on the church (the actual souls) not the church building or organization. We are charged with inspiring within them great confidence in God, so they can run with purpose and power (see Habakkuk 2:2; 1 Corinthians 9:24; Hebrews 12:1-2).

A business leader once explained that the best leadership is displayed when the people look around and say, "we did it ourselves." I say that in the church the best leadership is displayed when the people look around and say, "God did it through US." We have been empowered by God Himself to develop His church into a powerhouse that will spiritually set the world on fire. We have the choice to either empower people to greatness in God or to drive our own leader-SHIP in pursuit of personal glory. I hope you choose the former.

References and
Further Study

Abshire, David M. *Facing the Character Crisis in America*. Washington, D.C.: Center for the Study of the Presidency, 2006. http://cspc.nonprofitsoapbox.com/facing-the-character-crisis-in-america.

Cerna, M. "What Really Matters for Carrying out Successful Cross-Cultural Exchanges: A Comparative Study of Professionals from China and the USA." *International Journal of Business & Management*, vol. 8 no. 23 (2013), 130-148. doi:10.5539/ijbm.v8n23p130.

Cowan, S. B. and Spiegel, J.S. *The Love of Wisdom: A Christian Introduction to Philosophy.* Nashville, TN: B & H Publishing Group, 2009.

Dubrin, A. *Fundamentals of Organizational Behavior,* 4th ed. Mason, OH: Cengage Learning, 2007.

Henry, Matthew. *Matthew Henry's Commentary on the Whole Bible,* "Psalm 75." Peabody, Mass., Henrickson Publishers, 1991 (originally published 1706), http://biblehub.com/commentaries/mhcw/psalms/75.htm.

Hill, A.E. and Walton, J.H. *A Survey of the Old Testament,* 3rd ed. Grand Rapids, MI: Zondervan, 2009.

House, R.J., Hanges, P.J., Javidan, M., Dorfman, P.W., Gupta, V., et al. *Culture, Leadership, and Organizations: The GLOBE Study of 62 Societies.* Thousand Oaks, CA: Sage, 2004.

Jordan, J.M. *Living and Leading in Ministry.* Hazelwood, MO: Word Aflame Press, 2006.

Kouzes, J. and Posner, B. *Christian Reflections on the Leadership Challenge*. San Francisco, CA: Jossey-Bass, 2004, 85-98.

Lussier, L.N. and Achua, C.F. *Leadership: Theory, Application & Development*, 4th ed. Mason, OH: South-Western Cengage Learning, 2010.

Morgan, G. *Images of Organization*. Thousand Oaks, CA: Sage, 2006.

Northouse, P. G. *Leadership: Theory and Practice*, 6th ed. Los Angeles, CA: Sage, 2013.

Robinson, Edward, and trans. William Gesenius. Brown-Driver-Briggs Hebrew and English Lexicon, Unabridged. New York: Houghton Mifflin, 1905, http://biblehub.com/hebrew/4584.htm.

About the Author

C hris Olson is an ordained minister who has served in leadership and ministry roles at congregations of all sizes for nearly twenty years. He has more than fifteen years experience in business management and organizational leadership. Chris has a master's degree in organizational leadership with a concentration in organizational development consulting from Regent University School of Business and Leadership. Additionally, he is a published author, professor, and leadership consultant. His passion lies in teaching and developing systems and processes for Christian leaders.

Chris Olson is the co-founder of the Center for Apostolic Leadership: **www.apostolicleader.org**

The Center for Apostolic Leadership

**Developing Leaders... Igniting Revival...
Changing the World!**

Who We Are

Mission:
The Center for Apostolic Leadership exists to empower and equip churches with resources and training in leadership formation, strategic planning, and organizational development that will foster worldwide revival.

Vision:

To see worldwide revival come to pass through leaders developing leaders.

Services:

We provide both onsite and remote services with in depth models and materials to bolster your own personal growth as well as to develop church wide programs, policies, and procedures

Personal Leadership Development

Coaching and training designed to take your personal leadership skill to the next level. We design a customized, tailored program to fit your needs. Not every leader is the same, and not every leader needs the exact same focus. There is no "cookie-cutter" approach to true leadership development.

Development of Church-wide Leadership Formation Programs

Every strong church is characterized by strong leadership. Therefore, we find it imperative that churches be intentional in developing leaders; equipping and empowering them to be sent. Working with the senior leadership of your church, we help customize a plan for successful leadership development in your church.

Strategic Planning

All churches should be active in fulfilling the Great Commission. However, it is increasingly harder to do in this day and age without a strategic plan that will provide a road map for revival. Some plant, some water, and God gives the increase, but laborers must be spirit-led and purposeful in reaping the harvest (1 Corinthians 3:6; Luke 10:2; Matthew 13:24-30). We work with the senior leadership team to develop a strategic plan toward winning your city and making disciples of Christ.

Organizational Development

Strong churches are fortified by strong infrastructure. Our organizational development services analyze your church's leadership and reporting structure, types of ministries, and other important aspects making recommendations so they align with the vision, mission, and culture of your church. Everything we do creates and establishes culture, and that culture must align with the vision and mission of the church, both local and global.

Founders:

Dr. Amy Olson has served in leadership and ministry roles at congregations of all sizes for more than two decades, and has over fifteen years experience in organizational leadership and management. Amy obtained her doctorate in strategic leadership from Regent University's School of Business and Leadership, and is an internationally published author, professor, strategic advisor, and executive coacth. In addition to her passion for developing Christian leaders and teams, Amy enjoys playing music, traveling, and spending time with her family.

Chris Olson is an ordained minister who has served in leadership and ministry roles at congregations of all sizes for nearly twenty years. He has more than fifteen years experience in business management and organizational leadership. Chris has a master's degree in organizational leadership with a concentration in organizational development consulting from Regent University School of Business and Leadership. Additionally, he is a published author, professor, and leadership consultant. His passion lies in teaching and developing systems and processes for Christian leaders.

Contact us through our website at:

www.apostolicleader.org

Also available by The Center for Apostolic Leadership

The 3 Cords of Apostolic Leadership

A leader's Guide to Effectual Growth

Improve the impact of your church administration with this thorough study of leadership and organizational development. Experienced church leaders Amy and Chris Olson present a realistic approach to help you build a team with powerful direction.

The 3 Cords of Apostolic Leadership addresses three central aspects of church leadership:

❖ Spiritual disciplines upon which apostolic leadership is built

❖ Leadership practices, with in-depth models of servant leadership and transformational leadership

❖ Innovation, outreach, and team-building practices to improve the community aspect of your church

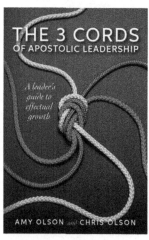

Whether you're new to church leadership or you're looking to improve a long-standing institution, you will gain clarity in how to empower every aspect of your church. From its spiritual core to the outer community, your church will grow from the inside out.

Order Today!
https://www.amazon.com/Cords-Apostolic-Leadership-leaders-effectual-ebook/dp/B071HWS4WT

Made in the USA
Monee, IL
07 April 2021